# Raising Children in Modern America

*WHAT PARENTS AND SOCIETY SHOULD BE*
*DOING FOR THEIR CHILDREN*

# Raising Children
# in Modern America

*WHAT PARENTS AND SOCIETY SHOULD BE
DOING FOR THEIR CHILDREN*

## Nathan B. Talbot, M.D.

*Chairman, Harvard Interfaculty Seminar on Children*

LITTLE, BROWN AND COMPANY · BOSTON · TORONTO

SECOND PRINTING

T 02/76

The frontispiece photographs are by FPG/Muller (top), and FPG/Haimes (bottom). The last photograph in the book is by Robert Adam.

LIBRARY OF CONGRESS CATALOGING IN PUBLICATION DATA

Talbot, Nathan Bill, 1909–
 Raising children in modern America.

 Bibliography: p.
 1. Children in the United States—Addresses, essays, lectures. 2. Children—Management—Addresses, essays, lectures. 3. Parent and child—Addresses, essays, lectures. I. Title.
HQ769.T265     301.43'1'0973     75-31571
ISBN 0-316-83136-0

*Published simultaneously in Canada*
*by Little, Brown & Company (Canada) Limited*
PRINTED IN THE UNITED STATES OF AMERICA

If there is anything that we wish to change in the child, we should first examine it and see whether it is not something that could better be changed in ourselves.

— Carl Gustav Jung

# Preface

In recent years it has become clear that the advances in technology which have added so much to the lives of so many in nations like ours have also resulted in new problems, some of which are as worrisome in their own way as those they have displaced. One of the reasons they are a cause for worry is that many are social and behavioral rather than principally material in nature. As such, they involve variables that lie outside the realm of the natural sciences, which have served as the wellsprings of these advances. Consequently, it has become increasingly necessary to broaden the scope of explorations to include the knowledge and skills represented in the social as well as the natural sciences. And related to these are disciplines such as education, economics, business, government, politics, law, the arts and so forth.

In our modern world, about the only organizational structures under whose aegis one can find all these gathered together are the nation's universities. One might conclude, therefore, that universities have an exceptional capacity to tackle complex problems in the round. Dispersed through their faculties are experts in all the above and often many other fields. Traditionally, however, the tendency has been for each group to keep to itself and to concentrate on searching ever deeper into the intricacies of its own particular field. This has been due in part to lack of a mutually interesting common cause of sufficient importance to justify the time and energies of a variegated group of experts over a period which was long enough for them to reach an understanding of each other's fields and to work together as a multidisciplinary team of problem solvers.

A few years ago I had reached the point in my work with children where I felt that such an approach was essential in order to solve many of the most troublesome difficulties currently being experienced by young Americans. Fortunately, quite separately, two of the senior administrative officers of Harvard University, Derek C. Bok and John T. Dunlop, had come to a parallel conclusion about the need for a multidisciplinary approach to the pressing problems being experienced by everyone living in modern America. Together, while serving respectively as deans of the Law School and of the Faculty of Arts and Sciences, they had sought and obtained support from the Ford Foundation for conducting a series of interfaculty seminars. Their purpose was to examine various aspects of these problems, and they had in mind that one of these seminars should be concerned primarily with children. As you can imagine, when I was invited to assume responsibility for organizing and leading such a group, I did not hesitate to accept.

Happily, colleagues on the Harvard faculty and many other experts outside Harvard expressed enthusiastic support for this project and willingness to commit many hours of personal time and effort to it. With the advice and support of the respective deans, it was possible to form a steering committee made up of representatives of the Harvard Faculty of Arts and Sciences (Jerome Kagan), the Graduate School of Education (Sheldon White), the Business School (Renato Tagiuri), the John F. Kennedy School of Government (David Mundel), the Center for Law and Education (Marian Edelman), and the Law School (Stephen Breyer), together with an economist-consultant on the roles of women as mothers in contemporary American society (Mary Potter Rowe) and me, representing medicine and serving as chairman. With this steering committee continually functioning to maintain a broad perspective in the project, we were able to enrich and enliven each session by having three or four individuals with special knowledge regarding the topic under consideration join us as ad hoc experts for that particular occasion.

Our first goal was to take a look at the whole range of problems currently being encountered in raising children in America from conception to young adulthood. This was done with a view to determining their origins and to posing some practicable solutions. Our second objective was to make our findings available to the public in ways that might serve to stimulate widespread discussion and constructive action by persons in all walks of life. This is one of two books that have been prepared in accordance with these aims.

The first book, which is being published simultaneously under the title *Raising Children in Modern America: Problems and Prospective Solutions,* sets forth the papers written by seminar participants in connection with the twenty-seven meetings held over the course of a year and a half. In planning these sessions, I as chairman talked with each principal author-leader to explain how his or her topic fitted into the total seminar framework. Each then prepared a preliminary paper, which served as a basis for three hours of discussion. This was tape-recorded and subsequently transcribed verbatim. Because the setting was informal and the number attending small — from twelve to fifteen people — discussion was uninhibited and therefore exceptionally rich in content of facts and ideas.

The names and titles of all those who contributed so effectively and generously to these meetings are listed in an appendix located at the end of this book. It will be found there that the 106 participants were representative of a total of 57 different disciplines and came from 45 different agencies or major divisions of large institutions. It will never be possible to acknowledge fully the importance of the contributions made by each one of these persons. This is particularly true with respect to members of the steering committee, who maintained an average rate of attendance in excess of 85 per cent, and in addition always responded generously to every request for special aid.

The first book is designed to give readers direct access to a cross-section of the information and ideas generated under the aegis of specifically named seminar leaders. In contrast, the present volume is intended to present a distillate of all the material garnered from all sources as it is viewed by one person. As the chairman of the seminar series, it was my lot to be that person. This has involved a considerable amount of selective filtering of the myriad facts and ideas represented in the position papers, in current books, periodicals and newspapers, in the transcriptions of seminar discussions and in personal conversations which I have had with many participants.

The preparation of this manuscript has also led to the formulation of some concepts and proposals for action beyond those discussed explicitly in the course of the scheduled seminar meetings. Accordingly, while I want to underscore the fact that I could not possibly have written this volume without the aid and support of these many other people, it would be unfair to hold them accountable for the material presented here. In these connections, I have frequently taken advantage of the writer's prerogative to use the word "we" to give an impersonal character to the text and to avoid the egotistical sound associated with repeated use of the word "I."

I would, however, like to use the first personal pronoun to express my special thanks to Jerome Kagan, Sheldon White, Robert Nelson, Guido and Faith Perera, Gerald Lesser, Lloyd Ohlin, Marian Edelman, Peggy Charren, Janice Milligan, Charles Dinarello, Robert Mulford, Richard King, Evelyn DelGizzi and my very able secretarial assistant, Penny T. Greene, for their willingness to give me the benefit of meticulous editorial advice. I also take pleasure in expressing appreciation to Mary Jane Walsh, Roger Donald and Elisabeth Gleason Humez of the editorial department at Little, Brown and Company for their many constructive suggestions and ever-ready support of this effort. My deepest gratitude is to my wife, Anne Perry Talbot, whose backing, encouragement and wisdom have been of immeasurable value to me.

Nathan B. Talbot
June 1975

# Contents

# Raising Children in Modern America

WHAT PARENTS AND SOCIETY SHOULD BE
DOING FOR THEIR CHILDREN

# I

## Setting the Stage

THERE are approximately 78 million children in the United States. This means that about one in every three American citizens are infants, children or adolescents. Those individuals represent the future of our country. It is a simple fact. If they're in trouble, we're in trouble. And there are multiple signs today that all is not as well as it should be with the youth of our land. Isn't it time for us to take a hard look at the status of our children, to learn from what is all right, to acknowledge and correct what is wrong?

On first look one might argue that things should be better, because with the technological and scientific advances of this modern world, some things *have* improved.

Take, for example, the matter of infant and child mortality. As late as 1900 to 1915, 27 out of every hundred babies born alive in the USA died in their first year. Another 12 per cent died before they attained adult age, thereby bringing the overall infant-child mortality up to nearly 40 per cent. In those days, prematurity, infection, nutritional disturbance, congenital malformation, heart disease or some other physical or biologic malady were the chief causes of death. But today, as a result of the great advances in physical health sciences, a child's chances of growing up to adulthood, if born alive in America, are more than 97 out of one hundred. If the child is born full-term and free from serious defects (as most children are), his chances are better than 99 out of one hundred. And he can look forward to a longer life. Since 1900, life expectancy has risen from an average of about forty years to more than seventy. Moreover, chronically disabling conditions such as tuberculosis, diphtheria, rickets, poliomyelitis, rheumatic heart disease and most of the other crippling diseases have almost become rarities in this country.

At the same time, scientific and technological advances have allowed man to use automated machinery to perform many, indeed most, of the routine tasks that he used to have to do by hand. And through the wonders of mechanization, material necessities and luxuries have become available to large numbers of people in generous quantities. Unemployment aid, welfare and social security systems have been established on a national scale to protect individuals against calamitous deprivation. In many ways, therefore, it would seem as if we should be experiencing the millennium of prosperity, security and human happiness which men and women have been dreaming about for centuries.

But this is not the way things have worked out. Our very successes have created new problems. Because changes have come so rapidly and been so extensive, we are having a hard time keeping up with the challenges they pose. Substantial numbers of children and youth are dying or becoming disabled as a result of causes which are primarily social and behavioral rather than organic in origin. Accidents have taken the place of infections as the leading cause of death among children. Suicides, homicides, illegitimate pregnancy and venereal disease are all on the increase. Infant and child abuse, juvenile delinquency and crime have soared. Large numbers of children run away from home each year. In the midst of affluence, millions of children are living in poverty, and millions are receiving such inferior education that they have relatively little hope of extricating themselves from the debilitating conditions in which they live. Many of these problems are crippling young people's chances for a bright future as much or more than did the physical ailments which used to be the greatest threat to their well-being.

This Harvard Interfaculty Seminar provided an exceptional opportunity to explore this matter in a comprehensive way. Our goal was to take a look at the whole range of problems encountered in raising children in modern America, from conception to young adulthood, in order to try to determine their origins and propose practical solutions. A tall order, indeed!

We started with the following basic assumptions:

1. Most human beings are endowed at conception with the potential for developing into reasonably healthy, competent adults. Only approximately 3 percent of our population give evidence of serious, genetically transmitted handicaps. We can therefore presume that failure to thrive during infancy and childhood in the vast majority of cases is the result of environmental deficiencies.

2. In addition to obvious physical necessities, human beings require a number of essential psychosocial supplies.

3. Human beings have a powerful, intrinsic tendency to maintain a healthy state by adapting to the environmental circumstances of their lives. Our built-in, automatic *homeostatic* systems have made it possible for men and women to survive the approximately two and a half million years that they lived on this earth prior to the advent of modern scientific public health and medical care practices.

4. Even though this adaptive capacity is extensive, it is nonetheless limited. Human beings are vulnerable to deprivation below certain critical minimal levels, and to toxic overdosage when pushed beyond their upper limits of adaptive adjustment. This applies to almost everything human beings come in contact with: water, oxygen, heat, vitamins, minerals, affection, attention and discipline.

5. It might be easier to determine the approximate location of these limits — and what the consequences of overreaching them are — if we focused on the key variables involved rather than on the myriad ways in which they present themselves in nature or in society. It is easier to grasp the concept of the body's requirement for water in terms of ounces of water than it is to think about the fluid content of all the water-containing foods and beverages we consume. Similarly, it surely would be easier to comprehend what kinds and levels of social input children need than to try to think about the many ways by

which input is transmitted in different cultures and under different conditions.

After pinpointing these five assumptions, we went wherever they led us. Early on, we were able to agree on what we believe to be the most basic human psychosocial needs, which we listed as:

1. being needed and wanted;
2. being attended to, cared for and protected;
3. being valued, cherished, accepted and given a sense of belonging;
4. being guided, educated, stimulated toward social capability and subject to limits of socially acceptable behavior;
5. being given opportunities to gain satisfaction in life through useful work and creative and recreational activities.

Supportive and constructive forms of psychosocial input are matched in nature by the opposites listed below.

1. being shunned or considered superfluous;
2. being neglected or abused (psychologically);
3. being maliciously belittled, hated, rejected, spurned;
4. being indulged;
5. being denied responsibility, or opportunities for independent thought and action; having everything done for one.

Even though these variables cannot be measured directly by physical or chemical means as their biophysical counterparts can, it usually is not difficult to recognize when a child is being grossly overburdened, deprived or actively injured. For example, infants and young children fail to thrive either physically, intellectually or emotionally when there is no one to spend time cuddling them, playing with them, or otherwise giving them personal attention. Yet as little as one hour a day of attention from a caring person can go a long way toward reversing manifestations of deprivation, just as a quart of fresh water and a few grams of sugar per day can make the difference between dehydration and death, or passably comfortable survival for a shipwrecked sailor awaiting rescue. Although we haven't measured it, we've seen the same thing with hospitalized infants who have responded to relatively limited amounts of affection from concerned members of the nursing staff. In these connections, it is interesting to note that the spread between minimal survival requirements and ordinary daily allotments is generously wide.

There is a lot we don't know about the psychosocial needs of children, but that does not mean we are helpless to improve their lot. Many of the major advances in preventive and curative medicine have been made on the basis of simple observations before people clearly understood why certain things worked. During the sixteenth century, while scurvy raged throughout Europe and on ships at sea, Jacques Cartier learned from Canadian Indians that his sailors would recover if given juices from the Almeda tree. This was two hundred years before the curative effects of lemon juice were demonstrated and almost four hundred years before ascorbic acid was isolated and the nature of Vitamin C was understood. Similarly, by heeding the comment of a patient that dairymaids who had had the cowpox seemed not to be vulnerable to smallpox, the British physician Edward Jenner was able to develop a vaccine against smallpox more than a century before the first virology laboratory was opened and scientists began to understand why vaccines give protection.

We are at the same sort of threshold in relation to psychosocial deprivation, intoxication and injury. We know a lot of ways to help children recover and thrive, even though we are not always sure how they work.

This book presents in condensed form the essence of all the material read, written and discussed during the course of the Harvard Interfaculty Seminar. It is intended to be a useful book, focusing on the identification of shortcomings in the way children are being raised in America today and on the development of ways and means whereby people in all walks of life can work to better the lot of children.

We will now proceed to present our findings and proposals, starting with the question of who should have children, when and how many, then working our way through the topics of filling the parental role, setting the goals for, and defining the content of, child rearing, methods of meeting essential developmental needs and, finally, the necessity of assuring that a job slot will be waiting for each individual. We will focus at least as much on the quality of living as on the duration of life, in the belief that life will not be viewed as an irreplaceable treasure for long by many unless it yields satisfaction to people while they are alive.

## 2

## To Have or Not to Have

OBVIOUSLY children are needed to insure the survival of the human race. So there is no question that human beings should continue to have children. But there are questions as to who should have them, how many to have, and under what circumstances.

There are many indications that in the United States and many other parts of the world, we have far more people than we can support physically or psychologically. This dilemma has not happened as a result of increased fertility, but rather as a consequence of the reduced mortality which we mentioned in Chapter 1. A very high percentage of infants and children now survive not only to reproductive age but into a prolonged period of adulthood and on into old age.

At the same time, the shift from an agrarian economy to a mechanized industrial society which has occurred during the last century has decreased the need for great hordes of people to operate farms and hand-produce the material supplies required to keep society functioning. This shift has tended to place children in the position of being more of an economic drain than an economic asset. Equally important, it is depriving many children of a major source of self-esteem; namely, being really needed by one's family or by society to perform necessary work.

It will be remembered that being genuinely needed is one of the basic requisites for successful human development and continuing happiness. In the pretechnical, preindustrial era children had lots to do in terms of chores which were essential to the welfare of their families. In meting out these chores, the parents' intention was not so much to build the child's character as to get done work which had to be done. The child obviously got a reward for this. He could see that he had a value.

Nowadays this kind of work has almost disappeared. As a result, if any work is assigned to children, it is apt to be "make-work" or "busywork" to a large extent, and more often than not it is consciously prescribed with character-building in mind. If the child does not appreciate the value of the work, he sees it as a kind of useless exercise.

Aside from the fact that this kind of work does not provide a child with the psychological and social benefits that the old-style chore did, it can also give him a bad attitude about work and its value to himself as a major component of life. Work is apt to become viewed, if not as a form of punishment, as a kind of ethical exercise which, being contrived rather than genuine, has little value. All this also points up the importance in society of making sure that there is a reasonable balance between the total number of people and the total number of job slots, space and resources available to meet people's basic human psychosocial needs.

Technological advances have also given mankind the ability to consume energy and other raw materials, occupy space, manufacture goods and create waste products at rates beyond almost everyone's wildest dreams. For example, during the 1960s, while the population of the United States increased 13 percent, the consumption of goods and services rose 60 percent, energy consumption 50 percent and the miles travelled by automobiles 40 percent. These advances have in turn enabled us to enjoy a standard of living that is far superior to that being experienced by most of the rest of the world, which might not be a problem if our nation were completely self-sufficient with regard to supplies of fuel and other essentials. But, we have learned recently, this is far from being the case and we are now having to face up to the fact that the rest of the world is not going to allow us to enjoy our luxurious living at low cost to us and little profit to them, while they continue to live a simple and, in some instances, almost primitive existence. This means that we cannot expect even to be able to sustain our present high standard of living unless we are willing to contain, possibly even reduce, our population over the years ahead.

Historically, long before modern contraceptive methods became widely available, people have curtailed their fertility when circumstances made it necessary or propitious. Sensing these changing circumstances, Americans have done likewise to the extent that we have reduced the average birthrate essentially to a one-for-one replacement level. But it will take another thirty to fifty years of continuously curtailed reproduction to accomplish a balance between births and deaths that will result in a zero rate of population growth. This time-lag is due to the current bulge in the number of persons generated by the post–World War II baby boom who will not have completed their period of fertility and reached the ends of their lives for several decades.

It seems to be quite clear to most people in the United States today that achieving zero population growth control is desirable and necessary for the proper and sane functioning of our society. But, encouraging as the overall drop in birthrate is, it has not solved one heartrending problem, namely that of the hundreds of thousands of children born each year who are not really wanted by their parents. Studies indicate that between 1966 and 1970, 14 percent of births in this country were undesired. This means that during these five years more than two and one half million babies were born who probably would not have been if the parents' preferences had prevailed.

This fact is important for more reasons than just maintaining a balance among total population, natural resources, space, jobs and other factors. Central among the most deep-seated, instinctive hungers infants and children experience from the day they are born until the time when they are fully on their own is the need for assurance that they are wanted and needed personally and that they will be cared for and protected by people who love them. Any child who is born undesired (and that is often the case in such instances) to parents who are ill-prepared to care for him or her is at an exceptionally high risk of experiencing severe emotional and developmental problems in childhood and later life. Indeed, as one expert on child-rearing has observed, many of these unfortunate youngsters are, for all practical purposes, "born to fail," and this is largely a direct result of lack of satisfactory environmental support. Prior to the liberalization of the abortion law in New York, 10 percent of the baby care centers in New York City during any given year were occupied by abandoned children.

One of the most extreme untoward results of unwanted pregnancies is child abuse — a growing phenomenon. The trouble here stems from the fact that children, being human, are not always easy to live with. When they get hurt or hungry or frustrated it is natural for them to fret or cry or lose their tempers, and at times this can try the patience of even the calmest parent. On such occasions it helps greatly to have chosen to take on the responsibilities of child-rearing. Unfortunately, these are the moments when a parent who did not want a child in the first place feels overwhelmed and may break down and vent his or her pent-up feelings of frustration and anger by brutalizing a youngster who not only may be totally helpless but also quite innocent of any serious misdeeds.

About 60,000 cases of child abuse are now being reported annually in this country and no one knows how many go unreported. It is estimated that as many as 50,000 children may die and 30,000 or more will be permanently injured as a result of abuse within the next ten years. The fact that the child's own parents are most often the abusers and are repeating a pattern about 90 percent experienced themselves as children makes these figures even more poignant. Even more startling is the probability that the youngsters who are being recognized as grossly abused physically represent only about one twentieth of a much larger group of children who are being neglected and abused psychologically by parents who are either too ignorant, indifferent, hostile or sick mentally or physically to give their children what they need.

It seems paradoxical that a society such as ours, which prides itself on being humane and supportive to the weak and downtrodden, has not been able to prevent criminal behavior towards its own children. However, if we take a close look, we can discern a number of possible explanations. One has to do with the attitudes, behaviors and value systems which our society as a whole holds with respect to human sexuality. Anyone who reads the news media, views movies or TV shows, looks at ads or reads modern novels knows how much the sensuous side of human sexuality has been emphasized in this country in recent years. With these models on public display everywhere one turns, it is no wonder that many persons, both young and old, have turned to engaging in sexual activities more extensively and in less inhibited ways than ever before in our history. And pregnancy by chance rather than by choice is a natural by-product of such behavior.

When one considers the circumstances surrounding such pregnancies, one finds that in a high proportion of cases the individuals were ignorant about ways and means of avoiding conception and many of them had little or no firsthand knowledge of what it means and what it does to one's own way of life to take on the responsibility of being a parent to a child.

One reason for this is that while nine-tenths of Americans believe that birth control information and materials should be made available to all men and women who want it, only six out of ten believe that contraceptive advice and materials should be made available to children. This is an age-slanted opinion. Eighty-five percent of those who are in favor of making information available to young people are between sixteen and twenty-one years of age themselves, but 44 percent of the people who are sixty years of age or over are against such an educational program. About a third of our population are fearful that explicit sex education for the young will predispose to more sexual activity and will not reduce the occurrence of illegitimate pregnancy among teenagers. This opinion appears to us to be anachronistic in view of the fact that between 1950 and 1968 illegitimate births increased from forty per thousand to ninety-seven per thousand live births. Nowadays, approximately one in seven American girls is having sexual intercourse by the time she is fifteen years of age, one in five by the age of sixteen, one in four

by seventeen, one in three by eighteen and one in two by nineteen years of age. And it is estimated that next year a million
babies will be born to American teenagers.

Unplanned and illegitimate births are occurring most frequently among girls and women who are severely disadvantaged
in respect to education and financial resources. While some of
these births are unwanted by their parents, some actually are
wanted for the very significant reason that having a baby comprises one of the few ways available to poverty-stricken people
to be creative personally. If one can't be rich in money, one
can be "rich in children." Unfortunately, this form of affluence
usually boomerangs and serves to perpetuate rather than overcome the deprivation from which it springs. Failure to recognize
and deal effectively with this problem comprises one of the
greatest weaknesses of our welfare system. Instead of enabling
and encouraging poverty-stricken people to become actively useful in a variety of necessary and satisfying ways, it is doing just
the opposite. This phenomenon must be faced up to because it
is unrealistic to think that those who are turning to pregnancy
as a way to satisfy their urge to be productive will cease doing
so unless provided with readily available, attractive alternative
ways to be creative. We will have much more to say about this
in later chapters.

Nearly 10 percent of all American females become pregnant
out of wedlock and almost half of the babies born out of wedlock
are born to teenage youngsters; only approximately one quarter
of first conceptions in this age group occur after marriage. Though
it may sound as if much of this behavior is promiscuous, surveys
indicate that this probably is the exception rather than the rule;
many of these girls are either leading a life of "serial monogamy"
or intend to marry the person with whom they are cohabiting.

To the foregoing we can add the sobering observation that
during the several years since the New York abortion law has
been changed, one third of the 193,000 abortions were performed
on teenage individuals. Twenty-four hundred of these were
performed on girls under fourteen years of age, 23,000 on fifteen-
to seventeen-year-olds, and a total of 65,000 on girls nineteen

years and younger. Also, one third of the young women who give birth to babies illegitimately are apt to repeat the act within two years. In some instances this is because they have not had a continuing source of instruction and support with respect to birth control. In other cases it is probably because they are so intent upon blotting out the unhappy memories of the first pregnancy that they do not return to the obstetrical unit for the follow-up visit in which it was planned to instruct them about contraception. This recidivism has been much lower among females for whom instruction and birth control has been made an integral and obligatory component of the therapeutic service.

In light of these grim facts, it is unfortunate that the law prohibits the dispensation of contraceptive advice and materials to children without parental consent unless they have become "emancipated" — that is, have left home to live on their own — have become pregnant or have contracted venereal disease.

The only practical way to eliminate ignorance as one of the major causes of undesired and undesirable pregnancies is to require that all schools, public and private, give courses on human sexuality. To avoid sensationalism and to insure a high degree of scientific accuracy and practical value, it is highly desirable that only instructors who have been certified as capable by some reputable agency — such as the National Center for Family Planning Services or Planned Parenthood — are assigned this task, the intent being to insure a satisfactory standard of competence and to avoid the inclusion of individuals who are inclined to focus on the erotic aspects of human sexuality. The inclusion of erotic subject matter is unnecessary in any program and is almost certain to arouse strong objections from conservative-minded parents, thereby placing the whole program at risk.

It probably will work out best if sex instruction in our schools is presented in two stages. The first should be for preadolescent grammar school pupils. At this time one can present basic facts about how babies are formed and where they come from without risk of arousing unmanageable emotions or desires. With this primary-level education as a basis, one can return to these same children when they are adolescent high school students and extend the instruction to include the information they need to avoid pregnancy and venereal disease. The latter type is sorely needed because the rate of occurrence of syphilis among fifteen- to nineteen-year-olds has doubled and the rate of gonorrhea has more than doubled in the last fifteen years.

To make the sex education sessions practically valuable, they should also indicate where students can obtain private advice about how to adapt available preventive measures to their personal needs. Since prevention costs much less than cure, it would be an economically sound practice for our society to assume the costs of all such services, thereby also removing financial barriers to their use by young people, many of whom have very little spending money.

Another major educational need is for children and youth of both sexes to be given opportunities to learn what it is like to take good care of infants and children day after day. When relatively large families were commonplace, many young people were expected to help their parents care for their younger brothers and sisters. We know from conversations with "graduates" of this homely type of training that most of those who have experienced it are determined not to become parents before they are thoroughly prepared for the task — physically, economically and psychologically. But when they do make the decision to become parents, one can rest assured that they have a pretty good idea of what they are taking on.

Recognizing that supervised experience in child-rearing is essential to understanding the implications of procreative relationships, a number of forward-looking schools have already inaugurated courses with academic credit for children who work as student assistants in developmental day care centers or in pediatricians' offices under expert supervision. The fact that many of these are heavily oversubscribed indicates that young people are very interested in this aspect of life.

In the final analysis, the question of whether one is to have or not to have a child almost always rests on the attitudes, behaviors and value systems of the individual persons concerned.

While it may be tempting to exhort sexual partners to think in terms of the welfare of the person they may be about to produce, either by choice or by chance, in the majority of instances it is probably much more realistic to urge prospective parents to think hard about what will happen to their own life-styles if they do conceive a baby. Though the custom frequently followed by clergymen and judges to give prospective marriage partners a brief talk on what marriage means, pointing out the difficulties as well as the fulfillments, is praiseworthy, it usually takes place too late to make any great difference. We would prefer that all children be given a course on what marriage and child-rearing are like as a normal part of the grammar and high school educational process.

We can illustrate what we have in mind by lining up some of the pros and cons of becoming a parent when one is less than eighteen years of age versus when one has attained full adult status. Taking the former first, we can say at the outset that it is hard to think of any really solid reasons for becoming a parent while one is still a child oneself. In fact, it is easy to think of a number of reasons for not doing so. For example, the facts show that the single most powerful indicator of whether a girl will extricate herself from poverty is the age at which she first becomes a mother. The lower the age, the worse the outlook, with the chances being nearly nil for those who are only fifteen or sixteen years old or younger. This problem is complicated by the fact that over 18 percent of the babies born to mothers under 15 years old are low-birth-weight prematures, which is twice the rate that prevails for mothers who are twenty years and over. Low birth weight predisposes to mental retardation, which, of course, adds tremendously to the burdens of a parent.

Because most teenage girls are largely unaware of these matters, substantial numbers are having babies either in the misguided belief that this is a good way to prove themselves, or to "get even" with their family or society, or to make up for the neglect they have experienced during their own childhood years. The sad reality is that pregnancies undertaken for any of these reasons are very likely to magnify rather than ameliorate the original problems. They also may contribute to the fact that 50 percent of marriages of teenage girls end in divorce.

Young people who have a strong and genuine desire to be with babies and little children should be provided with alternatives to having their own. For instance, they can be encouraged and helped to become skilled in child developmental care by working as mothers' helpers, day care center workers, nurses' aides and so on. However, we would like to emphasize here, as we will again later, that our nation is placing such a low value on child-rearing that it is failing to make this vital task seem as important as it really is to capable young people. One of the most challenging and important tasks facing us today is to change this misconception.

When one is talking about adults, though the principles remain the same, the issues take on different forms. On the one hand, it is entirely normal and natural for most adults to want the experience of being a parent at least once in their lifetimes. Certainly it is hard work and in many ways the most difficult and challenging of all human roles, yet it can also be one of the greatest sources of personal gratification. Even so, those who contemplate taking on this role should be aware that the chances that all will go well are less than one hundred percent. On the average, there are approximately 3 chances in one hundred that one's offspring will be seriously retarded mentally. Another 7 or so out of every hundred are liable to be handicapped by conditions such as diabetes mellitus, cystic fibrosis, congenital heart disease, accidental injuries or any one of a host of other miscellaneous ailments. While one cannot identify all of these early enough to avoid giving birth to a child who is likely to be handicapped, it has become possible to predict some things by means of modern genetic and other sophisticated fetal diagnostic measures. We urge, therefore, that all persons who have any reason to be concerned about such eventualities take advantage of one of the genetic or antenatal diagnostic counseling services which are now available in the medical centers of most sizable cities. Counseling should be started early — preferably before conception, or at the latest, during the early weeks of pregnancy. Then, if it appears advisable, pregnancy can be terminated legally and at minimal physical, psychological and monetary cost.

Of at least equal importance is the matter of temperamental fitness for being a parent. Most people probably are fit, but some are not. This can be because they have developed interests and goals which are so preoccupying that they have little time or energy left for anything as demanding as raising children. Or it can be simply that they do not like to work as closely with children as people have to if they are to fulfill their parental obligations reasonably well. Now when it has become essential to the well-being of our nation and the world to curtail reproduction, we find this type of thinking is dominating the minds of many young people, both married and single, who are taking great pains to make sure that they do not become parents before they are thoroughly ready, and then to have only one or two children at the most.

We endorse this position as being sound and in the best interests of all concerned. Prospective grandparents may feel frustrated and express disappointment at not having grandchildren to enjoy and to carry on the family name, and young couples may feel other social pressures to have children before they want to. Still, there is little doubt that our race is going to prosper much more from here on in if children are brought onto this earth only under circumstances where they are truly desired, where there is love, room and need for them and where they will have opportunity to live a decent life rather than merely exist.

No one ever need worry that this policy will result in a serious paucity of people. It has been demonstrated time and time again that human beings have a tremendous capacity to breed rapidly when the need arises. In fact, if there is ever a calamitous reduction in human population it will more likely be due to the side effects of overpopulation rather than to voluntary fertility control. This phenomenon is clearly evident in the animal world, where nature has set up a variety of automatic systems which come into play when a species gets too populous. The self-destructive behavior of lemmings, the loss of fertility among rabbits and the cyclical occurrence of lethal diseases among birds who have overpopulated are illustrative.

To summarize the thoughts set forth in this chapter, we believe that it is time to set aside old prejudices and taboos against instructing children about human reproductive function openly and frankly as they become curious about this subject. And when they are approaching the age when they will be capable of becoming parents, this instruction must be expanded to include the knowledge and resources they need to control their own fertility for the benefit of themselves and their offspring if they are to have one.

In practical terms, this will involve removal of legal and financial barriers to the provision of complete and accurate information and the prescription by physicians of contraceptive measures suited to the specific needs of individual child patients.

Adolescent students should also receive instruction and guidance about the realities and responsibilities of marriage and child-rearing, and, if they are interested, be given opportunities to practice child care firsthand.

Even in purely economic terms, these educational and service programs make sense. It costs only a fraction as much to prevent an unwanted pregnancy as it does to pay for the medical, social, educational and other costs of terminating a pregnancy, to say nothing of those inherent in rearing a child to adulthood. Since so many unwanted births occur in families who cannot handle the costs themselves — families too young, too poor or too ignorant to meet their children's needs once they are born — the economic burden often falls on society, that is to say, on taxpaying citizens who must support the necessary services. How many of the anti-abortionists, who insist on "the right to life" of every unborn child, are prepared personally to take full responsibility for the quality of that life from the day the child is born until he becomes an adult? In the final analysis, it is in human terms that the costs are most distressing. As a society we cannot justify indifference to the emotional damage inflicted on children who are neither needed, wanted nor valued any more than we can tolerate failure to cover their physical needs. The only way we can meet our obligation is by making sure that every child born into our society is wanted by parents who can and will take care of him. And when they cannot or are unwilling to, society must not hesitate to get to work early and take such measures as may be necessary to insure that the child will be under the care of an interested, responsible person.

# 3

## Filling the Parental Role
## Should Parents Do All the Parenting?

ALL children need at least one caring person who is willing and able to provide for their bodily needs and to protect and nurture them until they are old enough to fend for themselves. For normal healthy children, this usually takes sixteen to twenty years; for handicapped youngsters it can stretch out for an entire lifetime.

Most American children have been looked after primarily in their own homes. For years, many homes were so nearly self-sufficient in respect to raising their own food, making their own clothes, teaching and training by example and apprenticeship that the need for outside aid was largely limited to scholastic education and health services. Though sometimes limited in outlook and opportunities for variegated experiences, this type of home provided priceless opportunities to learn by doing and to develop a sense of personal value by sharing in the performance of tasks essential to the survival of the family. This environment also exposed children to the entire span of life as represented by the birth of younger brothers and sisters on the one hand, and by the end of life as represented by the decline and death of grandparents and other elderly friends on the other.

Many also felt the security that comes from belonging to a closely knit family of parents, brothers and sisters, with grandparents and other close relatives living either in the household or nearby. Almost half the households also included other adults whose presence was needed to run the family farm or business or to help parents in the housekeeping. Neighborly relationships were strong and almost everyone knew everyone else. And there were others besides one's immediate family that one could seek out as a playmate or as a friend in time of need. Consequently, many children lived under a protective network of concerned surveillance.

But as we know all too well, in the past fifty years these extended family and stable relationships have all but vanished for a large segment of our population. Even the nuclear family is at risk of being displaced by some new and less formal set of interpersonal arrangements. Paradoxically, most of these changes are by-products of the advances in scientific knowledge and technology which have led to so many improvements in our ability to nourish and protect our health and to ease the labors and enrich the experiences of mankind.

To illustrate this, we can recall the fact that mortality for the entire span of infancy and childhood has been reduced from 40-odd percent a century or so ago to slightly less than 3 percent today. And one third of these early-life deaths are due to inborn errors in body structure or function which are incompatible with satisfactory living. But in the period when these infant-child-mortality rates were high, married women had to devote most of their working lifetime to bearing and attempting to raise five, six or seven children in order to produce the two, three or more full-grown adults that were needed to run the family farm or business or meet the apparent national needs for manpower.

The demands upon women as housewives and mothers have been further reduced by the advent of centralized systems for supplying households with the material necessities of life and of many automatic laborsaving devices. It is also important to note that, as an almost unavoidable natural consequence of these technological "advances," the opportunities for women to satisfy their basic human desires for companionship, personal creativity and diversity within the framework of their homes have dwindled markedly.

Simultaneously, the position of men as husbands and fathers has been altered to a great extent. Many of those who were once supporting their families by diligent handiwork, skillful crafts-

manship or personally operated farms or businesses found it impossible to hold their own against the pressure of efficient,
technologically sophisticated mass-productive enterprises. So they
found themselves out of a job with a family to support. For most
of these men there was no choice but to move to one of the
nation's metropolitan areas in search of new means of livelihood.
And because large industries and business also experience changing needs, job opportunities kept shifting. This in turn made it
necessary for half of all Americans to change their home address
at least once every five years, a situation which eventually has led
to widespread dispersal of family members, rootlessness and what
has become for many a nation of strangers.

All these changes, however, added further impetus and new
opportunities for women, married and unmarried, to occupy themselves outside of the home in some satisfying way. Gainful employment was the obvious answer for most of them. The money
they earned was needed to balance the budget and to make it
possible for them to take advantage of the many tempting products rapidly developed by ingenious industrial inventors. Their
contacts with fellow workers provided the opportunities for social
intercourse which they needed to replace what they had previously experienced in busy households and close-knit neighborhoods.

Meanwhile, many husbands, finding themselves up against the
heavy competitive pressures of their places of work, felt it
necessary to spend considerably more time away from home
doing overtime, meeting job-related social obligations, traveling
for business and the like.

Twenty-five years ago, about one quarter of all women were
working for money outside their homes. By 1970, half were doing
so. Included in this group are 40 percent of all American mothers,
with 26 million children — of whom 6 million are less than six
years old.

More than a million children under thirteen years old are being
left alone at home in what is called "latchkey" status, to shift for
themselves while their mothers and fathers are at work. In Massachusetts alone, 20,000 to 30,000 of these children are under six

years of age! Though we lack detailed follow-up information on the fate of these children, we do know that many older youths who are arrested as delinquents give a history of having been grossly neglected by their parents. As a result they felt unattached, unwanted and unvalued. And, of course, they were essentially unlimited in their freedom to do as they wished. No wonder they got into trouble later on. The wonder is that our society has not yet taken steps to insure that no child be exposed to conditions likely to have such grave consequences.

Another several million children are deposited in day care facilities, most of which are not prepared to deliver good developmental care and loving personal attention. On the other hand, some businesses deserve credit for having established child care facilities close by the places where mothers of young children are working, and some of these are set up in such a manner that parents can either keep their eye on their youngsters while they are working, or at least be closely available if they are needed.

In view of the extent to which forces which used to hold families together have waned, it is not surprising that divorce has become more commonplace than it used to be. Today about one-third of all American married women have separated from their husbands by the time they are thirty years old, and another 10 percent split up eventually. The 800,000 divorces which are now taking place in this country each year are affecting the lives of nearly a million children annually and changing significantly the face of family life in America.

The vast majority of children in single-parent families are living with their mothers. This means that most are deprived of the care, protection and example normally provided by fathers. Nine out of every ten divorced women remarry. Sometimes the presence of a stepfather compensates for the absence of the natural father, but it can also result in the loss of the mother's attention, particularly if the stepfather brings with him his own children by a previous marriage. Also, there are sizable numbers of children in this country who are living in single-parent families because of illegitimacy, death or separation for other causes.

Another half-million or so are separated even more completely from their parents through placement in foster homes and institutions. Some of these children are well cared for, but many live for long periods in what amounts to psychological iceboxes, in which they have no contact with anyone who is intimately concerned about their welfare as dislocated human beings.

Finally, there is an as yet small, but growing number of youngsters under eighteen years of age who are being supported by the courts in their wish to live apart from their parents' home in "emancipated" status. Most have chosen to do so because they have found their home environment intolerable and would rather fend for themselves than live under the aegis of parents from whom they feel alienated. One wonders how often these same feelings led lads in days past to "go west" or "go to sea" in search of happier and more adventurous ways of living. In a sense, it is too bad that these challenging and colorful routes of escape have disappeared. Looking back upon them today, it would seem that they may have been more constructive outlets than those now open to "street youth."

All the foregoing observations point up the reality that forces loosed as by-products of recent advances in technology and industry have acted to diminish parent-child interaction in a large number of American families. We do not wish to imply that this is the case universally, however, for there are indications that many families have survived the stresses of recent times unscathed and are as strong and cohesive as ever before. For instance, as of 1971, 15,900,000 of the 48,125,000 married women in America had celebrated their twenty-fifth wedding anniversaries, and 1,200,000 their fiftieth. We do wish to emphasize, though, that even partial weakening of the role of parents has created voids in the lives of their children.

We can illustrate what we have in mind by taking the extreme example provided by observations on infants under care in orphanages during World War II when staffing shortages made it next to impossible for anyone to do anything more than keep them clean and fed. These babies simply failed to thrive physically, intellectually and emotionally. They failed to gain weight and tended to lie apathetically in their cribs, showing none of the vigor and responsiveness characteristic of the healthy young infant. Many succumbed to infections and other diseases which infants ordinarily survive. What is equally striking is the fact that as little as one hour of personalized attention five days a week in the form of cuddling, playing, talking to a child and the like by an affectionately disposed person miraculously changed such babies within a few weeks into alert, active, responsive and evolving little human beings!

Infants are, of course, totally helpless and unable to protect themselves, hence they are in many ways the most vulnerable. But children who are old enough to fend for themselves to some extent are liable to other forms of risk if they lack adequate supervision by their parents or parent surrogates. Being lonely and hungry for companionship, they are apt to wander astray in search of it and unfortunate things are apt to occur. Sometimes they join up with other children with similar problems and form a street community in which they all try to support each other socially. In circumstances where teenagers lack positive guidance and leadership from responsible adults, the increasing influence of the peer group and the street community can contribute to alienation from society at large. Many sociologists and criminologists consider this state of alienation to be a perfect milieu for the development of crime and delinquency. We will have more to say about this later on.

We see little to be gained by attempting to drive home harder the fact that even though most people realize that children have a very real and deep need for a secure parental person of some sort, many American children are lacking this essential element in their lives today. We therefore are challenged, individually and collectively as citizens, to face up to the task of making sure that this shortcoming in American child-rearing arrangements is overcome one way or another.

In tackling this, it is useful to bear in mind a few fundamental facts. One is that "old Mother Nature" deserves credit for having sustained generation after generation of human beings through infancy and childhood for all but about fifty of the approximately three to five million years that mankind is thought to have existed as such on this earth prior to the advent of modern scientific medicine. The initial phases of her success were due to the fact that human mothers were equipped anatomically, functionally and instinctively to nurse their babies during those first months of life when the infants were totally dependent upon human care and attention. To be sure, the fact that mother's milk is designed to fit their nutritional needs, is clean and directly deliverable at just the right temperature accounts in part for the success of this arrangement. But, equally important, the fact that mothers or wet-nurse mother substitutes were, for practical purposes, the only good source of infant nutrition guaranteed that some woman would pick up, cuddle and otherwise attend to infants' needs periodically during the course of every day. While it has been possible to substitute bottled cow's milk and other artificial formulas for breast milk as a source of nutrition for infants, no one has yet come up with a satisfactory substitute for affectionate, attentive, cuddling care.

The importance of this intimate parent-child contact has been underscored by Jerome Kagan's observation that infants start to form an attachment with those who placate them within a day or two after they are born. And they are reinforced by Harlow's studies on monkeys and chimpanzees. These have shown that separating babies from their mothers is not only unnatural, but is likely to result in a tendency for the babies to gnaw at their limbs, dash themselves against their cages and to ignore their own offspring when they themselves eventually become parents.

It is difficult for any natural parent or parent surrogate to satisfy the psychosocial needs of more than four or five children simultaneously. Studies have shown that children from large families often are adversely affected in both their educational achievement and their physical growth; their reading level is lower and they tend to be shorter than children who have fewer than three or four siblings. Thus, it seems likely that the psychological as well as the financial resources of parents are apt to become too diluted when there are numerous children. The trouble is that there aren't enough hours in the day for any person, whether rich or poor, educated or uneducated, to give more than a limited number of children the attention they need at critical periods in their development. Though this is unlikely to be a factor of importance in the now much smaller average American family, it may be worth remembering when setting up institutionalized group care arrangements.

Despite many superficial signs to the contrary, American society has continuously accorded the role of child-rearing an astonishingly low status in our national economy. Child care workers are not even listed as a category in the United States Department of Labor's *Table of Employment by Occupations.* Mothers' helpers and housekeepers stand at the bottom of the list of earnings by occupation. They receive less pay on the average than lumbermen, teamsters, fishermen and garbage collectors. When a mother who is left alone to rear her children turns to Public Welfare for supportive aid, the allotment she receives is at the poverty level. Regardless of how many children a mother is responsible for or how busy they keep her, she is not considered to be "working" in a way that contributes to the Gross National Product unless she is gainfully employed outside her home.

While we sympathize with those who wish to avoid policies which might make it more attractive to be carried on welfare than to struggle to earn one's own keep, we do not believe it is in the best interests of our nation to downgrade child caretaking roles to this degree or in this manner. There is probably no more difficult, and there certainly is no more important, task than that of raising children and we will suffer deeply as a nation if we fail to recognize this and reward it accordingly.

With the foregoing as a background, we can now take a look at several of the options Americans can choose among in striving to make certain that no child is left unattended by a committed, concerned and capable parental person. Of the numerous possibilities which one could conceive, eight appear worthy of mention. Please note that the order of presentation of these options bears no relation to preferences concerning them.

OPTION 1. *The classic, traditional nuclear family,* where the father works full-time as the family breadwinner and the mother works full-time at home raising a sizable number of children and managing a large household. In such families, both parents usually share in policy-making and child care, with most of the child-rearing done by or under the supervision of the mother. Whereas the procreation of large families made sense a few generations ago, it has become inappropriate relative to the present world situation. Yet, despite the obvious hazards of overpopulation, there still are some who feel that, because they are well-off financially or in a powerful position politically, they are "exceptional" and therefore should be free to have a large family if they want to. The trouble is that doing so not only sets a bad example to the rest of the community, but also intensifies the problems that their own children are liable to experience as a result of world shortages of supplies and jobs relative to population size.

OPTION II. *The modern nuclear family,* comprised of married parents and up to two children. The father contributes primarily as a wage-earner, policy-maker and night, holidays and weekend partner in child caretaking. The mother attends closely to her infants for the first months of life, but engages a competent mother's helper or homemaker to take care of the children during periods when they must be home-based while she is away at work. This can work out satisfactorily if she maintains freedom to remain home to tend to her children when they get sick or otherwise have special need for her.

OPTION III. *The androgynous household.* There is a growing trend toward sharing parental and other household and work responsibilities by young husbands and wives. This merging of roles, heretofore thought of as uniquely masculine and feminine, has been termed "androgyny" — a word in which masculine is represented by the Greek-rooted term *andro* and feminine by the term *gyn.* For the purposes of this discussion, androgynous life implies restructuring of work options between husbands and wives — as, for instance, by sharing jobs at home and out of home. The first couple to share an academic appointment at an Eastern college was regarded suspiciously. No one was sure it would work. Now — a year or two later — there are many such shared appointments.

This is in line with the fact that there already are millions of families in which the only parent or both parents work both inside and outside the home. One-third of the mothers in this country with preschool children are in paid employment, and at least a fifth part of the caretaking of these children is being done by their fathers. So it is entirely possible that if men and women become free to share financial responsibility, child custody, child care and homemaking, there will be many more househusbands, at least on a pro tem basis. Or, there may be more three-quarter-time workers, especially among young parents, if three-quarter-time employment becomes readily available for both men and women.

This has the advantage of enabling parents to care for their children between themselves rather than through surrogates. We believe that this could become a powerful force in recreating a sense of family solidarity, commitment and intrinsic strength. The chief difficulty here may be that only a few pairs of parents will be so considerate and unselfish that they are able to suppress ambitions and turn down personal opportunities for power and prestige in the world of work outside of their home.

OPTION IV. *Forms of communal, collective and cooperative living.* In recent years, young people who have been strongly out of sympathy with traditional social value systems and codes of behavior have experimented with various forms of socially atypical, communal households. There are tremendous variations in the substructure of these arrangements. Some are set up with tight sets of rules as to the manner in which people will relate, how the household will be managed, who pays for what, and so forth. Others are more flexible and function according to rules which are made and remade on a weekly basis in accordance with emergent needs, through some kind of democratic decision-making process.

One version of communal living consists in the "collective marriage" of from three up to eight or ten people. The group can be made up of members of one sex or of any combination of both sexes. Though some of these marriage ceremonies may be performed by radical members of the clergy, they are not sanctioned legally and so are not fully acknowledged by the public. Theoretically, the marriage partners share responsibility for the care of any children that they produce.

In another version, unmarried men and women collectively form a household where they live together, sharing everything, including themselves as sexual partners. If the persons who form this household do so for positive reasons, such as liking each other, believing that this is a better way to live, or the like, the chances of success may be fairly good. Children may thrive under these circumstances if they feel that they are firmly and securely attached to one parental person, be it a man or woman. On the other hand, the chances of success are low when people are escapees from traditional marriages and elect to live a communal life to avoid being lost souls in society or for other primarily negative reasons. Children reared in such households are apt to suffer from them.

Such exploratory manners of living are not altogether new, but represent an age-old tendency on the part of some members of every generation to want to revolt against the standards and styles set up by prior generations in one way or another. Historically, most have been short-lived. For example, the Mormon custom of polygamy has given way today to standard monogamous households. Harems, likewise, are going gradually out of existence, in great part because they are clearly unsatisfactory to the women members.

Another form of group living which deserves consideration consists in a cooperative arrangement wherein a number of married couples or single parents with one or two children have private apartments in a building which is equipped with common rooms where the parents can share and take turns in supervising and socializing their offspring. A variant of this is represented in old-fashioned neighborhoods where families living in separate homes share in preparing meals and, most importantly, in watching over their own and their neighbors' children. In effect, these schemes provide modern urban families with much of the sense of neighborly solidarity, mutual concern and shared purposes that once made it rewarding to live as a member of a congenial, extended family in a stable community.

OPTION V. *The single-parent household.* This is a rugged arrangement at best, especially for the parent. Moreover, it carries with it the obvious disadvantage of lacking the balance in point of view, life-style and so forth that derives from having both a father and a mother present in the home. At the same time, it has been demonstrated over and over that a single parent can raise children successfully. This is easiest when people live in well-established neighborhoods near other members of their own families. If they lack these, then it becomes important for them to have available occasional substitute parent arrangements in the form of excellent child day care centers, nursery schools and the like. Such services let them go to work where they can make contacts with other adults and thereby satisfy their own needs for human companionship, variety, stimuli and so forth. Single parents who lack this option are physically exhausted, socially starved and hard-up financially, to the detriment to their children as well as themselves.

OPTION VI. *Adoption and foster parenting versus family rehabilitation.* We see adoption as a close equivalent to natural parenthood provided only that the adoptive parents are well-endowed for the job and well-matched to their prospective charge. Foster parentage can also be very satisfactory when the match between "parent" and child is good and the situation is securely stabilized for the duration of the child's years of dependency. Unfortunately, in past years and still today, many foster placements are transient and insecure and hence unsatisfying to the child's needs. This custom has been based on the concept that one should do *everything* one could to get children back with their own parents and to avoid having children develop close personal ties with other parental figures. Now that it has become evident that many children are unwanted in their own homes, it has become clear that it is essential to their welfare that they be given an opportunity to grow up somewhere where they are wanted, loved and valued. At times it is administratively easier to accomplish this through placement of children in a foster home than it is to accomplish full legal transfer of parental responsibility by adoptive proceedings.

The life story of Harold, a man now forty years old, is illustrative. His father was a cab driver and his mother was a prostitute whom Harold's father put out on the streets to make money. When Harold was five and six years old, he was staying up until eleven o'clock at night selling papers around the City Hospital. At about this time the family broke up — his mother had a nervous breakdown and went to a mental hospital. Harold was sent to a series of foster homes.

After a while he began to steal and was arrested many times. At first the courts sent him to reformatories, but when it began to look as if he were incorrigible, he was sent to jail. One of his foster parents described him as one of the dumbest crooks he ever saw. What he did was to run out and steal something and then walk by the police station waving it in the air. As a result, he would be caught and put in a reformatory.

Harold is very attractive and likable as a person. He is attractive to women, too, and has married several times. A number of people have invested large amounts of time and money in setting him up in businesses. He gets money from people because they like him and because he looks as though he could be a success. He goes along in the business for a while, but then does something crazy — like slugging his partner or getting drunk. Then everything falls apart. The business fails and he is dead broke all over again.

When you sit down to talk with Harold about his seemingly self-destructive inclinations, he just goes over and over his childhood. Way down deep he thinks he's rotten — he thinks he's no goddamn good. But he's not. He's a rather decent person who is slowly killing himself.

The point is that Harold desperately needed to be part of a family where he could establish who he was and learn to feel good about himself. And here he is today a forty-year-old man, still trying to get back what he never had.

Part of his trouble was that the "system" failed to provide him with a stable substitute for his parents. Though one may encounter an exceptional nurse or governess or foster parent who becomes like a mother or father to a child, in general, hired people are not consistent friends. Day care workers are apt to have many other people to look after and maybe some children of their own as well. And they are responsible only during the periods when they are on duty and only so long as they are being paid for the services. Unless they have agreed to become permanent foster parents or to adopt a child, they have made no long-term commitment to the child. So when one encounters a child like Harold, who desperately needs to be part of a family, it usually is better to place him permanently in a congenial foster or adoptive home. *Unless* there are very solid reasons to believe that his natural parents can be rehabilitated in a short time, this is better than keeping him with totally ineffective or hurtful natural parents or placing him in emergency foster homes on a transient basis.

Henry Kempe, among others, has been demonstrating that rehabilitation can be accomplished in many disturbed family situations by arranging to have a qualified lay homemaker support the parents in the management of their home and children. At the outset this requires essentially all the homemaker's time and energies. A lot of effort is needed just to get the household functioning in a reasonably effective manner. But a lot more is expended in the form of personal attention, encouragement, demonstration and other varieties of social nurturance. The amount of time and effort needed usually begins to diminish after a few weeks and when all goes well can be reduced almost to zero within half to three-quarters of a year. Not only are the costs of this kind of family therapy relatively very low, but even more important, they have been found to be a much more effective means of straightening out home child neglect and abuse situations than placement of the child in foster homes or institutions.

OPTION VII. *Institutional placement.* This usually is kept as a last resort, except under circumstances when a child is so severely handicapped that the burden of caring for him at home is likely to destroy the rest of the family. Under these conditions, first-class institutional care — which means personal attention to the youngster by a trained individual at the routine caretaking level — can be a godsend to everyone concerned. This is likely to be more costly than most families can afford and so usually must be

underwritten by the community at large. The greatest danger
here is that children be misdiagnosed as hopeless and then more
or less forgotten for life. This can be avoided by thorough evaluation in the first place and by systematic review of progress there-
after. It turns out that certain mentally handicapped youngsters,
for example, can be trained to become partially self-sufficient
through performing simple but useful chores in the open community. This type of training is beyond the capabilities of most
families, but within the competence of institutions, as has been
demonstrated by the staff of the Fernald School of the Commonwealth of Massachusetts.

OPTION VIII. *Day care and other forms of parental back-up.*
Supplementary care has become one of the most pressing issues
in the entire American child-rearing complex. The reason is that a
substantial proportion of the millions of women who are mothers
of young children are working because they need the money.
However, many others are working or spending time doing such
things as helping out at the church or school library, playing in
the community orchestra and engaging in local politics in order
to broaden their social contacts and experiences beyond what is
possible within the confines of a small urban apartment or suburban home.

With three provisos, these out-of-home experiences can so enrich a father's or mother's personal life that s/he is better able to
serve the needs of the children than s/he would be if s/he
stayed home almost all the time. The first proviso is that the
children are well cared for while the parents are absent. The
second is that at least one parent continues to be readily available to the children for a minimum of one or two hours most
days. The third is that a parent (or permanent alternate) remain
the person responsible for the upbringing of the children.

The fact that both fathers and mothers are working or otherwise valuably engaged outside of the home base need not mean
that they are turning over the responsibilities of parenthood to
some sort of communal system. On the contrary, on the basis of
our experience with young working parents, supplementary child
care can solidify rather than disrupt the family and can improve

rather than hurt the children's chances for happy and developmentally rich lives.

Our reasons for taking this stand are multiple. For one thing, it is no longer possible — if it ever has been — for one parent to provide a child with all the attention, experience and guidance that is needed if he is to cope successfully with life in the now intricate American scene. This is no fault of the parent or the child. Life has become too complicated for any one person to understand and deal capably with all its major aspects singlehanded. Moreover, it has been demonstrated again and again that parental supplementation of appropriate quality can be remarkably valuable.

It would be hard to find a more striking example of this than that provided by the role of Annie Sullivan in the early development of Helen Keller, a child who was rendered both blind and deaf as a result of an acute infection very early in her life. Helen's parents supplied her with an abundance of love and solicitude, but were incapable of providing this extremely intelligent child with a means of communication. Neither were they able to supply her with the firm discipline she needed. Miss Sullivan's success in fulfilling these specific needs earned her the love and appreciation of her remarkable subject, as well as the title of "miracle worker" from an admiring world of onlookers. The miracle was not only that Annie Sullivan succeeded in reaching through the perceptual deficits that prevented Helen from communicating and led her to behave in an uncontrolled and extremely disruptive manner, but also especially that Miss Sullivan had the sense to appreciate the child's specific needs and potentials, and the strength to persevere until these were fulfilled.

Annie Sullivan lived and worked in that earlier era in American history when it was common for households to include one or more adults besides the parents. Homesteads were of generous proportions, and many more people could afford to hire household help than is the case today. Moreover, one knew most of one's neighbors, at least by name and often also as friends or fellow workers. Children growing up under these circumstances often had many opportunities to obtain attention, information, guidance and friendship from a variety of adults other than their parents.

This is important because the mere fact that a child is closely related biologically to his or her parents does not guarantee that children and parents are going to be congenial. Indeed, there is much evidence that certain children at certain stages of their development are so composed temperamentally in respect to being unhappy, crying, negative in disposition, irregular in the biological functions of eating and elimination, slow to adapt to new situations and intense in their reactions that they can fairly be called "difficult" — or, as they have aptly been labeled, "mother-killers." Parents too can vary in their inclinations and talents. Some are naturally suited to take excellent care of infants but are uncomfortable in dealing with older children or with adolescent youths. And some are just the reverse. Moreover, even the most staunch parent can become exhausted caring for a problematical child to the point where it is extremely hard to continue to deal patiently and wisely while continuously cooped up in close quarters with little or no support from family or friends. Much of the rising tide of child abuse is "brutality in the arms" which has resulted from pent-up tensions in a parent whose self-control has snapped in consequence of too close contact with an exhaustingly irritating child, with no external support or relief within sight.

One might suppose that the United States, with its ability to accomplish materialistic miracles and all its many evidences of concern for the welfare of those who are less powerful or less capable of protecting their own rights, would have led the way in devising means to assure that its children would be well looked after while their parents are away from home. Paradoxically, our nation has fallen way behind most others in this respect. Consequently, we still have what amounts to a "nonsystem" of day care and parental back-up resources in America. This is having an impact on the destitute, the working poor, the lower middle class and the middle class alike.

While it is impossible to give a precise figure concerning the total capacity of all American child care facilities, Marian Edelman, director of the Children's Defense Fund, estimates that there are approximately 900,000 spaces in *licensed* child day care centers in the United States today. This means that other arrangements must be made for the 25 million children who are now being cared for in *unlicensed* centers, day care homes, their own homes or other situations. When the Women's Bureau of the Department of Labor reviewed the situation in 1965, about half the children were being cared for in their own homes. The caretakers ranged from loving relatives, to fathers who were home by day because they worked at night, to paid babysitters, to older children who should have been in school, to incapacitated relatives. Hundreds of thousands under six were being left to fend for themselves unattended by any responsible person. In short, as Mary Dublin Keyserling concluded in a report prepared for the National Council of Jewish Women in 1972, the present day care system in this country leaves thousands of children with no care and hundreds of thousands in inadequate and sometimes destructive care. The researchers found infants and young children in abominable settings throughout the United States. Groups of young children were being kept in filthy basement rooms which had rats and broken windows. Others were being cared for solely by youngsters not even in their teens. In one center, licensed to care for no more than six children, one unassisted worker was looking after forty-seven children. To keep them under control, eight infants were tied to cribs and toddlers were tied to chairs. The worker then dealt with the three-, four- and five-year-olds as best s/he could.

Another center was very crowded and managed by untrained high school girls. No adults were present. Neither were there any decent toys. Rat holes were clearly visible. To keep discipline, the children were not allowed to speak.

And then there were some like Peter, aged three, who was left totally unattended by any parent in so-called "latchkey status." He had to get his own lunch, for no one else was home. He ate what he could reach and concoct, if he could get the refrigerator or cabinet doors open.

As Congresswoman Shirley Chisholm indicated in the foreword to Pamela Roby's book, *Child Care — Who Cares?* "Only 2 percent of the mothers in America are using day care facilities. Most of the rest face a nightmare of hodgepodge arrangements with elderly relatives, a rapid turnover of babysitters and bleak custodial parking lots euphemistically called family care centers. If you are lucky, a family care center means that your child will be safe, clean, fed and lovingly cared for by a gentle soul who likes children. More likely than not, you won't be lucky and in charge may be someone who is emotionally disturbed, uneducated, alcoholic, so old as to need help herself or all of the above."

This leads us to pose the question. What should and can we do about this major national shortcoming?

There are some excellent clues available as to how one can answer this first question. Some of them are based on observations and experience gained in our own country; others stem from the extensive work which has been done in other nations.

First, as regards goals, we subscribe to the thought that day care centers and allied parental supplementation arrangements for children in their preschool years should be designed to provide an environment which is adequate both from the point of view of bodily safety and nutrition, and with respect to the promotion of personal development and social adjustments. Moreover, they should give the child a sense of belonging to a community which is representative of the society beyond their immediate family that they will have to deal with on their own. For instance, they can learn how to adapt to new people and new situations and how to live cooperatively with children as well as with adults. They also can begin to learn how to take care of themselves. And they can be given chances to make contributions to the productive life of this miniature community and to learn how to participate in the work and play of the world outside the day care center. This can be done through cooperative play and by the assignment of responsibilities which lie within the children's range of competence. Moreover, their inner resources can be strengthened by allowing them to make discoveries with as little authoritarian guidance as possible and by encouraging them to be creative through painting, woodwork, role-playing as mothers, fathers, policemen and so on, as well as by participating in goal-directed peer group activities. These centers also provide a fine chance to instill early in life a conception of what it means to play fair, be just, be trustworthy and be concerned for the well-being of one's fellow humans as well as for oneself.

These are the kinds of goals which one finds in nations as diverse as England, Sweden, Norway, Nigeria, Israel, China and the Soviet Union. We find it thought-provoking that these are goals to which democratic as well as socialistic and communistic societies can and, to an almost universal extent, do subscribe.

We sense nothing in these aims which is necessarily in opposition to family solidarity, family loyalties, high ethical standards of behavior or happy interpersonal living. We mention this because there still are many in positions of power in America who would, in effect, like to throw the baby out with the bath water. They view a move in the direction of a national system of carefully designed child care centers as tantamount to making a communal approach to child-rearing over and against the family-centered approach.

At the operational level, for a day care arrangement to be of high quality the physical plant should have certain rather obvious attributes: spaciousness of rooms situated at ground level with satisfactory daylight lighting, adequate sanitation, indoor play space ideally of 35 or more square feet per child, an outside play surface of approximately 75 square feet per child. In addition, there should be cots for all little children to rest on, an isolated area for children who get sick, play and other equipment which is suited to the child's size and needs and which is attractive, solid, safe and easy to clean. To give children a sense of belonging, each should have his own drawer or cabinet for personal belongings. The center should also serve a nutritious meal and/or snacks if the children are there for more than a few hours.

Staffing arrangements are also of the utmost importance. There is general agreement that those in charge of infant and child care facilities should either have had at least two years of academic training and practical experience in the major facets of child development and care or have demonstrated special competence in dealing with young children. After extensive thought and careful review of this role, the Office of Child Development of the United States Department of Health, Education and Welfare published in 1973 a guide for training staff for service in day care, Head Start, nursery school and other preschool programs.

The following is an abbreviated and partially paraphrased representation of the six major areas of competency expected of "child development associates" trained for these roles: (1) Setting up and maintaining a safe and healthy learning environment as regards the organization of space into appropriate functional areas which allow for active movement as well as quiet engagement. (2) Advancing physical and intellectual competence through experiences which encourage exploring, experimenting and questioning and which lead to gains in the mastery of bodily acts, language, the use of numbers, self-expression and understanding of how things work, grow and so on. (3) Building positive self-concepts by providing an environment from which the child derives a sense of belonging to a community of children and in which which he or she can be given responsibility and opportunities to learn the elements of cooperation. Here the child development associate must know how to recognize behavior which is reflective of emotional conflicts around trust, possession, separation and rivalry and to adjust the child's program in ways which will strengthen his capacity to deal with these problems realistically. (4) Arranging opportunities for children to work and play and share responsibilities with adults in a spirit of enjoyment. In association with these, limits of acceptable behavior must be established. (5) Bringing about optional coordination of home and center practices and expectations with due respect for the cultural backgrounds of the families being served and with a view to recognizing and utilizing the strengths and talents of parents that may contribute to the development of their own and other people's children. (6) Keeping track of the child's progress physically, behaviorally and cognitively, with the aim of identifying signals indicative of possible problems and of making such changes as may be necessary to meet a child's particular needs.

In addition to these areas of knowledge and skill, training programs for child development staff members should cultivate sensitivity to children's feelings, readiness to listen and to adapt adult language as necessary to communicate with children, the ability to protect orderliness without sacrificing childish spontaneity and the capacity to maintain control without being threatening, to be emotionally responsive and take pleasure in children's successes while also being ready to be supportive when they have troubles or failures, to encourage imaginativeness and to bring humor into the group and to feel committed to maximizing the strengths and potentials of each child in relation both to himself and his family.

Parents as well as appropriately selected junior high and high school students of both sexes should be encouraged to participate in these child care activities. If they are properly supervised by trained child development staff, this type of participation can give youngsters an opportunity to serve others and to learn something about what it means to care for and be responsible for little children, and then give young people a realistic basis for dealing later in life with their own children when they become parents.

We stated above that as many or more infants and preschoolers are cared for at home as at day care centers of various sorts. This type of care, too, can be satisfactory, at least for a few months, if arrangements are adequate. For instance, we know of several young married couples, in which both husband and wife are working full-time, who have managed to find a young to middle-aged woman who has had extensive experience either helping to raise a family of younger brothers and sisters or raising a number of her own children, who enjoys working with infants and young people, who is warm, steady, happy, outgoing and principled and who is looking for full- or part-time work. Provided that the parents and the prospective home-helper like and trust each other, a very satisfactory arrangement can be developed. Typically, on workdays the mother or the father may feed or otherwise attend to the child's needs first thing in the morning before leaving home. The home-helper cares for the child for the balance of the working day. One of the parents then feeds the child his or her supper and, depending on his age, may put him to bed for the interval while the two adults have their dinner. After dinner, the child is again picked up and given personal attention for another hour or two. On weekends, both parents spend the bulk of their time with their child or children. And when they go on a trip, they are apt to take their children with them.

It was surprising to us to learn that some of these parents have uneasy, guilty feelings of shortchanging their children. We believe that there is no need for them to feel that way, because this can be a very good arrangement for all concerned. The chief shortcoming lies in the fact that children who are being raised in this manner may lack opportunities to live and grow up with other youngsters. It is partly for this reason that we feel that, as with other life necessities, it has become essential that excellent community child care facilities be made universally available. Those who can afford to pay the full cost should do so and those who cannot should be aided by the community at large.

According to Mary Rowe, the cost for a desirable level of preschool day care approximated $2,400 per child per year in 1972. If day care were to be made available to all, the total cost would probably amount to somewhere between $15 and $30 billion annually, depending upon the proportion of children who were being cared for on a part-time rather than a full-time basis. This expense is in contrast to the $850 million of United States government funds which was spent for such services in 1971. It also is in sharp contrast to the situation obtaining in certain other countries. For example, Israel, which in 1969 had a gross national product of $1,663 compared to the United States gross national product of $4,604 per citizen, was providing kindergarten for all five-year-olds, child care for half of the three- to four-year-olds, and comprehensive neighborhood mother and child clinics for over 90 percent of all infants and mothers.

There remains the practically crucial question: what price are we paying for taking this parsimonious stance regarding child care in the United States? Viewed from a nonmaterialistic standpoint, it has become recognized that neglect of little children leads to a lack of sense of family closeness, to feeling rejected and to lacking a sense of self-worth. As children grow older, this predisposes to all sorts of asocial and antisocial behavior — drug abuse, stealing, truancy and dropping out of school, sexual exploitation, illegitimate pregnancies and so on.

Even at an average price of $2,000 per year for fifteen years (total $30,000), the expense of providing for an individual child who is at risk of maldevelopment because of inadequate parental care appears small relative to charges for managing a mentally handicapped child ($4,500 to $8,700 per year), educating a youth out of delinquent behavior ($2,000 to $9,000 per year), housing him in a correctional institution or placing him in security care ($10,000 to $15,000 per year), or carrying a person as a dependent adult for approximately fifty years (total about $100,000). Today this whole gamut of problems among children is being reflected in the cost of crime to Americans which at the latest count has risen to over $84 billion a year.

We feel compelled to conclude that America cannot afford to continue to let leaders who are not responsive to these issues, as was the case with Richard M. Nixon, when he vetoed the Comprehensive Child Development Act of 1971, prevail any longer. This act had been passed by a vote of 63 to 17 by the United States Senate and by a majority of 210 to 186 by the House of Representatives. The act was the result of the assiduous efforts of a consortium of women's groups, labor unions, poverty and civil rights lobbyists, churches, educators, community citizen organizations, developmental psychologists, pediatricians and other leading child advocates. The *Washington Post* called the bill "as important a breakthrough for the young as Medicare was for the old," describing it as "a vehicle for a new national effort to make childhood livable."

The fact that Mr. Nixon's veto was not overridden by the Senate and House simply reflected the reality that there was not sufficient awareness on the part of the American public as to what we stand to lose if we continue to skimp on our national child-rearing priorities in favor of a whole slew of such other matters as voyaging to the moon, building supersonic transports and even to feeding the unfortunates of other nations whose uncontrolled procreative activities have led to mass starvation. The point is that we are engaged in a totally different, and almost totally novel, ballgame as far as raising children is concerned. The problems they are exhibiting today are products of the environment in which they are being raised.

There are signs the nuclear family may be on the way out and the extended family which used to ensure that the parental role would always be filled one way or another is a thing of the past. But the child's dependence on and need for a secure parental person or persons has not changed. He must have someone he can count on as a continuing source of guidance, protection and care. Fortunately, there is much to suggest that this someone can combine being both parent and wage earner. For such an attempt to be successful, there is high need for an extensive network of developmental day care centers, kindergartens and other services which, staffed by persons who are qualified by training and by temperament to function capably, can serve as parent surrogates during times when parents are away from home or disabled by illness or the like.

We simply must work in all ways possible to awaken people at all levels to recognize that we are shortchanging ourselves and the future of our nation by failing to invest in our children as our best and most critically important asset, just as we have and still are investing in nuclear fusion, laser beams, electronic computers, pollution control and so forth. One of the best places to start investing is in the areas we have been discussing in this chapter. In a word, child care is worthy of a position close to the top in our national hierarchy of priorities.

# 4

## What Infants and Young Children Need
## from Parents and Others

As we all know, this is a global subject and hence one which touches on a variety of closely related functions. Bearing this fact in mind, we have chosen to open the topic by assuming that certain of these functions are stabilized in a satisfactory state. Then we can consider other functions in some detail in a relatively simple and direct manner.

For instance, we shall assume that the child has one or another of the types of responsible parent described in the preceding chapter. We will further presuppose that both parent and child are basically sound in body and mind. This does not mean, however, that the parent is necessarily well-prepared by education or experience to perform the multiple tasks inherent in being an adequate parent. But we will proceed on the assumption that parents do work fairly closely with their children. We think that doing so may be in some ways as important to children and parents as mother-offspring relationships are to other species.

For example, Lorenz's observations demonstrate the existence of a critical period of a few hours' duration during which stimuli which conform to certain innate specifications will release following behavior in young goslings and ducklings. Following behavior on the part of the young birds in turn elicits nestling behavior by the parent, which results in the formation of an irreversible social bond. In birds this kind of imprinting creates the mechanisms by which the newborn locates its mother and its species.

Without assuming that these observations are directly transferable to human parent-infant relationships, we can say that the extent to which a child's parent may influence the ways in which the child evolves is determined in considerable part by the degree to which the child develops a sense of attachment to the parent early in life. The more social interaction an infant has with a person, the stronger his attachment to that person becomes. In most infants attachment behavior to a preferred person develops during the first year of life; and there is a possibility that there is a sensitive period, starting sometime after the sixth week in that year, during which attachment behavior develops most readily. Once a child has become strongly attached to a particular person, he is apt to prefer that individual to all others throughout childhood, even when separated from him. So, we would urge all parents to bear this in mind in planning for the care of their offspring during this initial phase of childhood. This is a period of unique opportunity in that it allows parents to become the first people to whom the child has a deep attachment. Equally, if not more, important, the events of the period may have a profound influence upon the degree to which parents become deeply committed to serving the best interests of the child.

As far as the child is concerned, as we have already stated, we can take it for granted that in better than 97 out of every hundred instances, a baby who is born alive and free from obvious defects is inherently capable of developing into a healthy, competent adult if adequately cared for, nourished and protected during his early years. In these connections it is interesting to note also that infants are equipped at birth with some remarkably effective internal regulatory systems. With few exceptions, these systems determine the color of their skin, eyes and hair, the shape of their face, their ultimate height and most of the other myriad details that make almost everybody, except identical twins, physically unique. Even identical twins may display some small differences as a result of random mutation of a gene or two. Though one cannot do very much to improve children's body configuration, there are many ways in which it can be warped or damaged; for example, by underfeeding to the point of emaciation, by overfeeding to the point of obesity, or by traumatically injuring it.

The situation is quite different when it comes to children's personality development. As was the case with their externally visible physical makeup, children are born with a brain which in some ways is comparable to a highly sophisticated computer, which has among other things an almost infinite capacity to store information and a unique ability to program itself in various ways. The fact that babies display a variety of essentially automatic, instinctive behaviors such as breathing, crying when hungry or uncomfortable, evacuating waste when necessary, smiling when content and when pleasantly stimulated shortly after birth indicates that their brains have already been partially programmed in certain basic ways.

Babies also display temperamental differences from the day they're born. These are reflected in differences in thresholds of responsiveness to being touched, moved or spoken to, in the intensity and manner in which they do respond, in their spontaneous activity levels, in the rhythms of their sleeping and feeding patterns, in their general mood and so forth. Also tucked away in latent, potential form are various talents. These talents, to a greater extent than most of the foregoing, must be nurtured and stimulated environmentally. For instance, not everyone is inherently blessed with a capacity to be a mathematician, or a concert pianist, or, for that matter, a cook, a housekeeper or a parent. But it is safe to assume that all normal people are endowed with the latent capacity to function well in some valuable way or ways. Parents, teachers and others can be instrumental in awakening inborn aptitudes and in enabling and encouraging the child to develop them. But a potential Artur Rubinstein could never realize his fitness to become one of the world's greatest pianists if he never heard any music and had no way of knowing what kinds of sounds can be obtained by the action of skilled fingers on the keyboard of a piano. At the same time, we hasten to add that no one can become a Rubinstein in any field without spending an enormous amount of personal effort in the cultivation of his talent.

Some may feel that all the educational and guidance efforts of parents and others serve only as activators of inborn potentials and so are not *per se* formative of character or skills in the evolving child. On the other hand, there are others — and we are among them — who see many indications that the value systems and ways of thinking and acting represented to children by parents and other meaningful people can exert a powerful influence upon them. The old line that the sins of the fathers are visited upon their children is perhaps no longer true in terms of venereal disease or in terms of a belief in curses and so forth. But we see again and again instances where the effects of parental neglect, abuse and amoral attitudes and behavior are being transmitted down the family line from parent to child. This may well be at the foundation of the mushrooming social and behavioral problems that we are experiencing in society today.

We know of no more compelling example of this than the observation that about 95 percent of the parents of abused children give a history of having experienced abusive treatment at the hands of their parents when they were children. This particular example is representative of a severe deviation from the norm regarding the provision of one of the five clusters of essential psychosocial supplies — in this case, protective care. Not only is protection lacking, which would be a simple matter of deficit, but in addition it is replaced by its direct opposite: namely, abuse.

Other less extreme examples are provided by observations on the effects which exposure to different cultural values can have upon the behavioral characteristics which children develop as they grow up in their home environments. This is nicely illustrated by the observations made by Beatrice and John Whiting on the nurturant-responsible versus the egoistic-dependent-dominant dimension of the behavior of three- to eleven-year-old children reared in six widely dispersed cultures. Three of these — Tarong in the Philippines, Juxtlahuaca in Mexico and Nyansongo in Kenya, East Africa — were representative of relatively noncomplex societies. In these, all the family heads were subsistence farmers. Settlements were composed primarily of dwellings with few, if any, specialized buildings such as stores, churches or fire stations. These communities depended primarily on an indigenous political system where authority was localized, and caste systems and priesthood were absent. Children reared under these circumstances behaved in a predominantly nurturant-responsible manner. This was evident in counts of the frequency with which children offered help (as by tendering food, toys, tools or helpful information) or offering emotional support in response to another's crying, fright or discouragement. In these cultures, helping mothers care for infants accounted for one quarter of the children's task assignments.

By contrast, in the three other communities — Khalapur in India, Taira in Okinawa and "Orchard Town," a New England town — an appreciable number of family heads were making their living at some occupation other than farming. In "Orchard Town," for example, the family heads were businessmen, professionals or self-employed entrepreneurs. In all three communities, the settlement was complex in that there were schools, fire stations, stores, churches and other specialized structures, and in that the political system was remotely centralized. While over half the children reared in the simpler cultures were engaged regularly in various necessary chores and tasks, comparatively few were so occupied in the more complex societies. The only chore in which more than half the children of the more complex societies participated was cleaning and sweeping; very few were assigned responsibility for the care of infants. Thus, these children had relatively few opportunities to gain the feeling of personal worth and competence that comes from doing chores and tasks which are clearly important to the daily lives of other members of one's family or social group.

Children growing up under these circumstances behaved in predominantly egoistic-dominant ways as by seeking help or support, by selfishly demanding or seeking attention by such direct requests as "Look at me," "See what I have done." These observations strongly suggest that the learning environment can exert a powerful influence upon the behavioral characteristics children develop as they grow up.

While types of social behavior are intentional, they may originate from within or without. Newborn babies react to pain and hunger by crying. This type of behavior is egoistic in that its purpose is to attract attention. It serves as a mechanism for obtaining the relief needed to reduce the baby's drive for help. The fact that a baby's crying is unpleasant to hear is apt to induce the caretaker to go to the baby's aid. If the baby then stops crying, the person who has done the helping is reinforced in his inclination to help the infant. This reaction may be further strengthened if the infant also breaks out in a captivating smile in response to his caretaker's attentions.

However, most of the tasks assigned to children do not have this type of built-in reward-response system. Consequently, the drive for most nurturant-responsible chores and tasks stems initially from parents and others who require that children do certain things at the peril of severe punishment if they fail to carry through responsibly. With passage of time, however, this kind of behavior may become internalized to the point that it becomes part of the child's personality. The end result may be behavior which is altruistic in that it is based on an intrinsic sense of concern for the welfare of others, coupled with a desire to be helpful.

As mentioned above, nurturant-responsible behavior and egoistic-dependent-dominant behavior comprise the antipodes of one of the major dimensions of human behavior. Both components of this dimension are important, the indications being that egoism may be as important to survival in complex societies as primarily nurturant behavior is to life in simpler societies. However, if egoism becomes so extreme that people have concern only for themselves irrespective of the effects of their behavior upon others, then everybody is at risk of losing not only the support of others which everyone requires from time to time, but also the sense of personal worth, involvement and security which comes from interpersonal exchanges of help. In other words, we believe that it is important in societies like ours to temper egoism with a modicum of altruism, just as it probably is necessary to temper nurturant behavior with a modicum of egoism.

In the simple societies mentioned above, many children were expected to — and did — function in nurturant ways by the time they were *three years old!* The question is "How can we accomplish this in modern America?"

It seems to many of us that we have lost a productive function for children in our society. And yet we realize that one of the best ways, and perhaps the only really effective way to get children to be human and decent toward others is to make sure that they are taught, expected and encouraged to be responsible for the nurturance and care of other people from the time they are very young.

This is by no means an original or unusual thought. For example, in her recent survey of contemporary child-rearing practices in China, Ruth Sidel learned that one of the basic dogmas enunciated by Chairman Mao is that children be taught to love and help each other, and care for one another.

This thesis is implemented starting as early as one and a half to three years of age. For instance, in nursery schools if a child falls down the teacher says, "We have to help each other," and then encourages the others to help the fallen child get up. Similarly, in the winter Chinese children wear jackets with buttons up the back. Since they cannot reach their own buttons, they help each other button up. After a while this way of thinking and behaving becomes a habit.

Youngsters three to five years old likewise are assigned "work" to do in the form of aiding others in need of help. Thus, when teachers have a bright child who has more energy than he knows what to do with, they assign him the task of helping one of his slower classmates with schoolwork. Five-year-olds are set to work in their classrooms wiping off tables, sweeping the floors and other tasks that have to be done by someone. They also plant seeds and grow edible vegetables. Through doing this, they begin to appreciate the effort that goes into growing the food they eat. Once a week they may be asked to spend half to three-quarters of an hour helping to produce something that has monetary value. For instance, a group of them may sit at a long table folding and filling boxes with crayons for export. There is no competition and no pressure to produce. The factory leases the work out to the kindergarten and pays according to the number of boxes filled. The money thus earned is used to buy a television set or other resource for the children.

Certainly such elementary forms of youthful work and service are well within the competence of modern America. What is more, we know that closely similar roles have been devised and implemented in some nursery schools and kindergartens in our land. But they are by no means universal and appear, if anything, to be declining rather than increasing. The question, therefore, is not so much "Can we devise ways and means for our children to learn what it means to 'work' and to help and be helped by one's fellows?" as "Are we prepared to treat this matter as one deserving of careful thought and high position on our national agenda of child-rearing priorities?"

There are other ways in which societies differ with respect to the behaviors they wish to cultivate or suppress. For instance, in modern America people are expected to express some degree of anger and hostility toward persons who are trespassing upon their property or otherwise violating their rights to personal privacy. Accordingly, it is generally acknowledged that parents should not always punish mild displays of anger or aggression by their children. On the other hand, if the Utku parents of Hudson Bay were to take this stance, they would be in serious trouble. The reason is that they live in three hundred square feet of living space for nine months of the year. Under these tightly restricted conditions there is no room for displays of anger, hostility or aggression. Consequently, these mothers consciously start to inhibit these types of behavior in their children from the time they are two years old. The result is that by the time these children are nine years old, they show none of the behavioral manifestations of anger that are so commonplace among American children.

It is of great importance to view things in relation to surrounding circumstances. We first became aware of this phenomenon one day when we attended a university seminar on perception led by Edwin Land, founder and president of the Polaroid Corporation. As the meeting was drawing to a close, he had the hall completely darkened and then projected two lantern slides on a standard screen. The first image consisted simply of a small square of black at the center of a large white square. The second was the opposite — a small white square surrounded by black, or so it seemed. In actuality, the small black and small white squares were identical images of a mid-value gray color — "mid" in the sense that the gray value stood just halfway between pure white and pure black. We *perceived* the gray to be white when it was surrounded by black and to be black when it was surrounded by white.

As Jerome Kagan has emphasized, this phenomenon has important implications in regard to child-rearing. One is simply an extension of the foregoing. Suppose, for example, that a child who has been thoroughly conditioned to behave somewhat aggressively in accordance with the contemporary industrial-urban "norm" is suddenly transported to Hudson Bay to live with the Eskimos. Abruptly, he finds that the ways he has been taught and encouraged to behave are in sharp *conflict* with those considered essential to satisfactory life in the Arctic. This type of conflict often leads to conscious worrying, to feelings of guilt, to accident-proneness and other so-called neurotic symptoms. These reactions indicate that the attitudes and behaviors which parents and others train into children can become a deeply rooted component of their personality. They also remind us that behavioral patterns which appear to be abnormal may actually represent a normal reaction to an abnormal or highly stressful situation.

We should like now to consider the degree of freedom that parents may have in teaching their children a given set of social or ethical values. We can illustrate by comparing the ways in which families living in different cultural environments and circumstances attend to and care for their offspring. In Nyansongo, Kenya, East Africa, mothers carry their infants on their backs or keep their babies close by under the immediate care of someone else by day, and sleep with them in their arms at night. These babies are almost never left alone up to the time they are weaned at two or three years of age. During this interval they are offered the breast without delay at the slightest indication of disquietude, hunger or discomfort. However, even though mother-child contact is close and nearly constant, it is unusual for these mothers to look at or fondle their offspring. Much of the same kind of care has been observed among Okinawan families living in Taira, Filipino families living in Tarong and among the Mixtecans of Mexico. The same is true among Indian infants living in the isolated highlands of Guatemala.

By contrast, in Khalapur, India, mothers have their infants sleep with them at night, but during the daytime when not in need of food or immediate attention, the babies are placed in cots, which are completely covered with quilts or with sheets as protection against insects and envious glances.

In eastern Holland, Dutch mothers have their infants sleep in canopied beds in separate, unheated rooms, the doors of which are kept closed. Because the mother also keeps the door to the room in which she is living closed, she is not always able to hear the baby cry. This practice is in keeping with the Dutch attitude that crying is a normal part of infant behavior, is good for the lungs and is not, therefore, always something to stop. Consequently, in the first ten months of life, infants in the eastern part of Holland are held only when they are being fed at three- to four-hour intervals. Moreover, they have no toys, no mobiles and only minimal stimulation. Consequently, the amount and variety of adult contact experienced by Dutch children is far less than that encountered by their average American counterparts. Yet, by the time they are five years old, there is no evidence of major differences in fundamental intellectual competence or effective vitality between the children who have been brought up in these differing ways. This finding strongly supports the notion that people can get across to others the idea that they are fond of them, concerned about their welfare and so forth equally well in a myriad different ways.

Thus we are finding that it makes a great deal of difference *what parents and others choose to transmit* to their children in the line of psychosocial supplies, ideals, ethical value systems and the like. On the other hand, it makes relatively little difference *how these are transmitted.* Provided they are reasonably consistent, the means can vary within widely separated but nonetheless real boundaries. As with material supplies, continued shortages or gross excesses in the provision of social supplies sooner or later result in the development of observable evidences of stress, malfunction, disease or disablement. It follows that one can rest reasonably sure that one is doing all right by a child if he appears to be physically and behaviorally healthy. On the other hand, one can be equally certain that things are not all right if a child — or anybody else — displays signs of dis-ease or disability physically or mentally.

These warning and danger signals can be of many sorts. It would be out of place here to attempt to list them in any detail. At the same time, it may be useful to mention a few of the more commonplace behavioral manifestations. These include such readily recognizable manners of behaving as hyperactivity, easy distractability, apathy, excessive shyness and isolation behavior, verbal abusiveness, physical cruelty, recklessness, self-punishing or suicidal behavior, disobedience and negativism or excessive conformity or dependence, destructiveness, dishonesty, running away from home, drug abuse, overeating, undereating, insomnia, hairpulling, compulsiveness, phobias, perfectionisms, scholastic underachievement. The same is true if a child appears not to be well-adapted to his family or to the community in which he is living, or is experiencing severe emotional distress with loss of ability to work, play or love, is incapacitated in regard to learning and problem solving, or is preoccupied with daydreams, delusions or hallucinations and, hence, is out of touch with reality.

Under the latter circumstances especially, parents should seek professional help promptly. However, under most other circumstances, they can safely take the time to examine the situation with a view to identifying major shortcomings and to devising ways to eliminate them.

For example, there can be a lack of awareness on the part of the parent of what children need from him or her in the line of psychosocial supplies. Sometimes the parental person is unavailable to the child because of being overwhelmed with intrinsic personal or extrinsic interpersonal problems of living, such as illness or poverty. Some also are in the unfortunate position of having a personal aversion or dislike for children in general, or for a certain child in particular. Sometimes simply thinking through a list of this sort may result in an awareness of shortcomings which can be remedied without recourse to outside help. Otherwise, parents should not hesitate to seek the kind of skilled help that can be obtained through the pediatric and family health care facilities that now are generally available in metropolitan areas, if not in rural communities.

In *sum,* as we review the topics touched upon in this chapter, a few stand out as being especially meaningful. Of highest importance are the choices made by parents and others with respect to loving versus hating, accepting versus rejecting, working versus loafing, being kind versus being cruel, being constructive versus being destructive, honest versus dishonest or self-disciplinary versus self-indulgent in their ways of thinking and behaving. Children usually can sense a mile off which way balances are being tipped in their parents' own inner ways of thinking, deciding and behaving. Maybe this is why it makes so little difference just how parents and societies choose to transmit their value systems and behavioral preferences to their children. The ways do not have to be exact as long as they hit somewhere within the target they are aiming for. It may not even be essential to express overtly something as fundamental as a feeling of affection for another by kissing, embracing or other explicitly overt actions. Indeed, careful observations on mother-child interactions have disclosed that successful American mothers may exhibit this type of behavior less than 1 percent of the time they spend with their children. In other words, it is the basic feelings and intent which underlie all the things we do and say to and with each other that tell the story. When our children are in trouble or we are in trouble with them, it is essential that we search our own behavior and value systems for causes and solutions.

# 5

## What Older Children and Adolescents Need from Parents, Schools and Society

THE task of raising children in modern America becomes increasingly diversified and challenging as we move away from infancy toward the middle years of childhood. Though this diversification may seem at first glance to be quite amorphous, in reality each of its constituent parts is related to the provision of the basic material, social and cognitive supplies mentioned at the outset of this volume. Moreover, all are designed to help children become capable of living in society and able to enjoy life. We continue to bear in mind that social standards differ widely, not only among cultures but also from family to family and from time to time within cultures and families. So it is worthwhile for parents and their surrogates to draw distinctions between matters that are really crucial and those that are rather minor, and hence not basically consequential to society or to the health, welfare and development of the child.

It is also important to make sure that children have reached the point in their development where they can understand and respond to training efforts. For example, it has been found that children are better able to respond to toilet training efforts after they reach an age of fifteen to thirty months than they are prior to that time. Likewise, it has been learned that it is difficult, as Sheldon White has said, for "parents to enter children's heads" before the children reach the age of six or seven. In so saying, we are referring to children's ability to assimilate adult concepts of right and wrong, good and bad and things of that sort.

With these thoughts in the background, we would like now to outline what appear to be the salient components of the child socialization-education-training process during the middle years of childhood. In doing so, we are not striving to be all-inclusive. Rather, we are hoping to be able to indicate to our readers the breadth and depth of this task under a series of separate but intrinsically related subheadings.

*Social amenities.* At its beginnings, socialization is concerned largely with types of behavior which have an immediate bearing on pleasant, convenient living. Reverting for a moment to infancy, we can cite toilet training as a universally applicable example. Prior to training, most infants and little children are totally uninhibited in responding to the internal stimulus to defecate occasioned by distention of the large bowel beyond a certain point. When the parent punishes the child for moving his bowels under circumstances other than those considered acceptable or desirable, the child begins to experience anxiety. The next step is for the child who feels the urge to defecate also to feel anxious about avoiding any punishment. Toilet training has been accomplished when this anxiety leads him to delay moving his bowels until he is seated on the toilet. All this is fine if all goes well. But it may be disastrous to the development and maintenance of a positive parent-child attachment if the training is undertaken before the child is old enough to learn readily or if punishment is overdone to the point where the child becomes extremely anxious.

It follows that the way in which these early socialization efforts are managed sets the stage favorably or unfavorably for subsequent attempts by parents to cultivate desirable, and to suppress undesirable behavior in their offspring. Therefore, it is important to note that many of the goals of socialization can be attained by the opposite mechanism of reward, in the form of praise and encouragement to children when they behave in socially desirable ways. This approach has been studied and applied by people like B. F. Skinner, who has even been able to train pigeons to do complicated things when rewarded instantly for desired behavior. It has also been used by neuropsychologists in training mentally handicapped children to do such desirable things as clothing themselves, keeping clean and doing simple, useful tasks.

Other social amenities, such as courteous behavior, being socially poised, sincere, honest, unperturbed and nondisruptive, likewise involve the cultivation of inhibitory mechanisms. They also are heavily dependent upon having human models to emulate that children can respect and admire. For example, children are not likely to inhibit temptations to use foul language if they hear one or both of their parents cursing and swearing when upset. Similarly, children rarely pay much attention to admonitions to curtail eating sweets and other rich foods if the parents themselves are overweight and regularly indulge their appetite for food.

*Communication skills.* Second on our list are efforts aimed at the ability to communicate through the use of language, the written word and mathematical symbols, all of which have become of elemental importance to success in modern America. Though one might suppose that all American children would be attaining these basic skills, there are more than a few who have not learned to speak, even by the time they are three or four years old, simply because they have been isolated and neglected. And there are literally millions more citizens who cannot read or write well enough to fill out a driver's license application blank or a welfare form. Neither can they comprehend simple directions, a TV program guide or ordinary newspaper headlines. Nor can they express themselves well enough verbally to gain acceptance as employees or as citizens.

The reasons why so many lack even the elementary education needed to render them able to speak, read and write English and to solve elementary arithmetic problems are multiple. In part this is a historical phenomenon, for we have not yet attained the universal education our nation set out to achieve at the turn of this century. In 1912, the average teacher had only a seventh-grade education, so it has been necessary to educate and train teachers as well as pupils. But the biggest problem has been and still is that a lot of youngsters are not in school and never go to school.

According to the analysis of the 1970 United States Bureau of the Census data on nonenrollment, made by the Children's Defense Fund, nearly two million children seven to seventeen years of age were not enrolled. Of these, nearly half were under thirteen years old. There are ten states which have more than 6 percent of school age children not enrolled; in Michigan 8 percent of white sixteen- and seventeen-year-olds and 14.5 percent of black youngsters were out of school. Moreover, as a result of talking to thousands of parents and children, school officers and community leaders, the researchers came to the conclusion that the two million figure represented in the United States Census data reflected only the surface of the problem.

Not included in these were the hundreds of thousands who were expelled or thrown out of schools for disciplinary reasons, the truants who eluded the census takers, those whose parents did not answer the census questions accurately because they did not understand English, the handicapped and pregnant youngsters who were allegedly, but not actually, receiving home instruction and those whose parents were ashamed to tell stranger census takers about members of the family who were mentally retarded, emotionally disturbed or otherwise embarrassingly handicapped.

Though out-of-school children come from all racial and income groups, there is a tendency for those with low-income and unemployed parents to be disproportionately nonenrolled. The same is true of those whose families have less than an average educational background or are members of minority groups. These trends, of course, tend to perpetuate illiteracy.

In addition, the researchers encountered a variety of school-imposed barriers which effectively prevented children from attending school. For instance, in one Kentucky county, 21 percent of the children who were found to be out of school indicated that they were unable to pay for textbooks or school fees; some also were out because they lacked decent clothing. Then there are the many children with special needs because of physical, mental or emotional problems, who were labeled handicapped, judged as uneducable and denied entry to public schools. When the Children's Defense Fund staff analyzed the data submitted to the

Office for Civil Rights in 1973 by 505 school districts in Alabama, Georgia, South Carolina, Mississippi and Arkansas that had children in classes for the educable mentally retarded (EMR), they found that the probability that a black student would be in such a class was five times that for a white student; in ten of the districts, the probability was ten rather than five times. Moreover, even though less than 40 percent of the total enrollment was black, over 80 percent of the students in EMR classes were black. Furthermore, it is estimated that there are four million limited- or non-English-speaking children in America. Only a tiny proportion of these are enrolled in bilingual educational programs, and a significant number are not attending any school.

The use of suspension and expulsion for disciplinary reasons was also commonplace in the Children's Defense Fund findings. Thus, in the five states of Arkansas, Maryland, New Jersey, Ohio and South Carolina alone, during the 1972–1973 school year, at least 152,904 children were suspended at least once for an aggregate of over 4,700,000 school days — the equivalent of 3,200 school years. More than a few of these suspensions were arbitrary and basically unfair — for example, one child was expelled for the rest of the school term (three months) because he could not pay the $5 to replace a ruler he had broken accidentally in a shop class.

The impact which these problems are having upon the lives of children and others is exemplified by the following briefs culled from the many reported by the Children's Defense Fund.

*Racial discrimination in classification.* Janice, sixteen, is in the tenth grade in Macon, Georgia. She has been suspended several times for refusing to be placed in a special education class. The root of this problem extends back to September 1972, when Janice says she was told by her white advisor that she should be placed in special math and English classes because of her "attitude." Janice refused on grounds that these classes are for "dumb people." Since September, she has been suspended on an average of once every three months for refusing to be placed in these classes. However, she has continued to return to school in her regular classes and maintains a C average. Janice feels she needs tutoring in math and English but does not need to be placed in a special education class. If she is forced into such a class, she will drop out. She would be ostracized by her friends who would tease her about being in a class with a "bunch of dummies. Teachers in these classes don't teach, they just try to keep the dummies quiet."

The threat of being placed in this class has caused Janice to "study harder in order to show the white folks that she is not dumb." Thus far, Janice has not been suspended this school term. However, her white counselor told her that she should be in a "special school or in reform school." This advice caused her to come home crying. She is building up a "great deal of hostility toward all white people and often talks of the good days at the all-black school."

*The exclusion of children with special needs.* Billy was born with spina bifida. When he reached the age of six, his mother tried to enroll him in the Children's Center program in Montgomery, Alabama. They refused to admit him. "They told me they didn't have enough help with his Chux [diapers]." He has not been to any school in four years. She never had any contact with public school officials. "I want him to have some kind of learning, to learn how to communicate better. Why can't he have the same opportunity the other two [her normal] children have? He's human too."

*The exclusion of children for language reasons.* Fernando is now nineteen. He came to Springfield, Massachusetts, from Puerto Rico when he was fifteen. He could not read or write in Spanish, as he had never been to school in Puerto Rico. He was put in the fifth grade. He got no bilingual instruction, so he stayed home because he could not understand what was going on. A truant officer came to get him and told him that if he did not go to school and did not want to be put away, he would have to go back to Puerto Rico and stay with his father there. He did. He returned to America when he was eighteen. Fernando said that he did not like school because he "did not know how to read or write or understand what was happening and they wanted me to read and write." His mother used to send him, but he did not want to go — he used to stay at home.

*Prejudice on school-age marriage and pregnancy.* Pregnant girls are not required to leave school; but "if they show a great deal, we don't force them out but we kind of advise them" that it might be difficult for them. ". . . It is hard for them to ride the school bus or to sit in the classroom."

—Last summer, the Autauga County school system in Alabama was sued by a married student who was prohibited from playing football. He won, and they now allow married students to participate in any extracurricular activity. Concerning this the Superintendent of Schools said, "There's no policy on married students, except the girls have to maintain their maiden names until they graduate, for our record keeping."

"We prefer that married students don't attend. This is a district-wide policy. I don't know why" (Junior High School, Denver, Colorado).

*Lack of enforcement of compulsory attendance provisions.* The following are samples of parents' response when asked whether the compulsory school attendance laws were being enforced.

"When a child is out of school, no truant officer ever comes around to find out why the child is not in school. That's what they're getting paid for so they should do their job."

"The kids who aren't even present in class get marked present because the schools get paid for it."

"I see 12, 13, 14-year-olds and they're not in school. Some never go at all and the ones that are enrolled only go when they feel like it. Next door there's a 16-year-old boy who hasn't been in school for two years. And another one just got suspended and I don't think she's going at all. Nobody cares."

"My daughter cut class for one month and I didn't know anything about it until she was suspended."

Sadly, these actions not only deprive children of the educational opportunities they need so desperately, but they also compound this loss by humiliating them publicly and by essentially guaranteeing that they will grow up to be illiterate and, therefore, largely unemployable. This situation automatically breeds rebelliousness, delinquency and permanent dependency, at very high cost financially and otherwise to society as a whole.

Certainly these are inexcusable shortcomings in American child-rearing arrangements. Moreover, it is a protracted tragedy inasmuch as people learn in a stepwise fashion. Each step forward makes the next one easier. Each step lost when a child is ready to learn retards or permanently hampers the whole process. This is one of the reasons why the Head Start program, which was formulated to eliminate gaps in basic cognitive experience early in life before children enter school has been such an important effort on behalf of the long-range well-being of disadvantaged children.

However, Head Start has also had its problems. We concur with Sheldon White's contention that its chief shortcoming has been that it was never implemented as originally intended. The trouble stemmed from the fact that Head Start was set up as a national program in the brief span of six months, and the easiest thing to do under those circumstances was to set it up as a preschool system only. The original mandate, however, called for health care, for coordination of services in the community, for work with the family and for community action programs. In other words, it called for a lot of things besides raising children's I.Q. Instead of following these directives, Head Start was managed under the assumption that people in the program knew better and could do better than families and they superseded them. The original attitude held by many on the staff was "Let's keep the parents out. The family is spoiling the kids; they're not stimulating them, they're not talking to them. We experts should take these children and give them reasoning skills and vocabulary." But these teachers soon found that they couldn't move a foot; indeed, they couldn't run the program without involving the family.

Efforts are now being made to overcome these deficiencies in services to children through diversifying them and through working *with* rather than *around* the family. Despite its many difficulties, Head Start has been moderately successful in doing things that are not strictly speaking educational — that is, in supporting the family, in creating liaisons between schools and ethnic minority communities and in socializing children who are out of the mainstream of our American culture. As a result, the program continues in political favor. At the grass roots level, parents react strongly to any threat to discontinue the program in the neighborhood. And centrally, even in this period of appropriation cuts, the budget for the program has been upped slightly to about $500 million. All this is encouraging, for it goes to show that grass roots public opinion, if properly coordinated and channeled, can have a powerful influence on governmental priorities.

This is worth bearing in mind as we consider ways and means to overcome the basic problems of just getting children to school and setting them up in such a way that they can learn the elements of speech, reading, writing and arithmetic, and above all gain a sense of joy and satisfaction from participating in the learning process.

In these connections we consider the recommendations for action proposed by Marian Edelman and her associates at the Children's Defense Fund to be rational and reasonable. In brief, they are urging legislators to eliminate charges for essential educational services and materials which make it difficult for poor children to attend school, to feel welcome as a peer and to take full advantage of their capacity to learn. Children should be kept in regular classrooms to avoid placing them in unnecessarily downgrading and humiliating situations which predispose to lack of self-respect and a sense of discouragement and futility. At the same time, care should be taken to identify special needs with regard to transportation, clothing, nutrition, health, language, sight, hearing and so forth and arrangements should be made for the provision of such special supports as may be required to meet these needs.

To alleviate unwise, unfair or arbitrary misclassification of pupils, parents should be involved in the classification procedure and have an opportunity to participate in decisions regarding the management of their children. It appears also to be both advisable and necessary to have the Health, Education and Welfare's Office for Civil Rights (OCR) monitor the whole process with a view to insuring that children are given a square deal at school as regards exclusion, special placement, discipline and so on.

*The physical and natural sciences.* Because we have reached a point where we are beginning to push the limits of our physical world, it has become more important than ever for children to know about the physical and biological characteristics of their own bodies and of the earth they live on. It is also essential for them to understand the fundamental natural laws that govern our environment and our interaction with it. A good many people over many generations have assumed that as long as scientists understand these things, superficial knowledge was enough for the rest of the people. This is no longer true, because action by an informed citizenry has become crucial to bringing about the controls and changes that are needed to make certain that our homeland will remain strong and our world habitable for our children's children in the years ahead.

*The social and behavioral sciences.* In a society which has become as interdependent as ours, it has become essential for children to understand the characteristics of their social world and the basics of human relationships. Children need to learn at an early age, among other things, to serve as a source, as well as recipients, of the psychosocial supplies we have been concerned with in these discussions. This is one of the deepest of all human obligations and, at the same time, one of the greatest sources of satisfaction in life. Children should also be helped to recognize the immediate and long-range effects of their choices and their behavior upon others. With this knowledge as a base, they should, in due course, be led to understand the characteristics of their social world and the essence of social interactions, governance, politics and social order.

*The humanities.* One of the most worrisome characteristics of many of today's young adults is their lack of any sense of history. Lacking knowledge of what has gone before, they keep rediscovering ideas, ways of living and so forth that have long since been tested and found wanting. Lacking this background of knowledge, they fail to foresee the far-reaching, often predictable consequences of their own and other people's decisions and actions. Survival itself may depend ultimately upon whether children learn enough about the whole course of human history to be able to recognize and avoid circumstances which are likely to lead to the destruction of men and nations, and on the other hand, to appreciate and cultivate those which truly enhance the quality of life on earth for everyone.

This survival involves training children's minds to reason and make judgments based on careful analysis of relevant information, the identification of major issues, the marshaling of pertinent arguments on all sides of a question, the elimination of those that rest on faulty reasoning and, finally, arriving at conclusions soundly related to these facts and arguments.

In saying this, we are urging that attention be focused more on the end effects of major social, behavioral and materialistic phenomena than on the usual chronologically systematic, historical record of significant events. For instance, we undoubtedly could learn much of value about the dangers inherent in certain of our present social trends from studying a good analysis of the attitudes and behaviors which preceded the decline and fall of the Roman Empire. The same might be said of an examination of the social situations, human perceptions and ethical value systems which led to the American Civil War and World Wars I and II. Likewise, it could be profitable, in view of the impending shortages of vitally important natural resources, to characterize the faults in thinking that have led men and women to exploit the forests, fields and rivers of our land to the point where huge tracts of productive territory have been turned into deserts, much natural beauty has been irretrievably lost and many fascinating and valuable species have been decimated.

If the impression held by our literary colleagues is correct, books specifically designed to present human history in these terms to children and young people either are not widely known or else have not as yet been published. It is hoped, therefore, that there are historians who appreciate the importance of presenting facts impartially in ways which make their relevance to modern-day living compellingly evident, who will be interested in preparing source material suitable for regular use by grammar and high school students. It is hoped also that the many schools which have omitted history from the core curriculum will reassign enough time to this subject to insure that oncoming generations will have some awareness of what can happen if one behaves one way or another. It is also important that young people have some idea of the hard work, indeed struggle against great odds, that has gone into creating the masterpieces and institutions that we value most highly.

*Training for service.* Thus far we have been concerned largely with conveying information essential to reaching wise decisions. Translation of these into action involves training in operational skills accompanied by opportunities to practice and, eventually, to help others who are in need of help to be useful and creative in socially valuable ways. Such activities, in turn, form the basis upon which children build their sense of personal identity, self-esteem and self-sufficiency.

If these attributes are to become deeply ingrained, it is important that they be fostered early in childhood. To start with, the child needs to see these kinds of behavior modeled by people whom he loves, respects or admires. In addition, the stage must be set in such a way that these kinds of activities appear to be normal components of life — not just "busywork" designed to keep children occupied in some innocuous way. Though this stage setting poses more of a problem to parents living in modern America than it did to many of their forebears who were raising children in agrarian or pastoral surroundings, as we have mentioned before, nonetheless parents today have found that there are many ways in which it can be accomplished satisfactorily in relatively simple ways.

For example, in Viet Nam, starting at the age of four, children are engaged in cooperative play. They need each other for the kind of playing they are doing, and hence through playing they

learn the elements of mutual supportive giving and interdepend-
ence. As is illustrated by remarks made by a woman experienced
in child-rearing abroad, this has not yet become typical of child-
rearing in the United States. She states: "I went to St. John's
School [a preschool for working mothers] and there were children at round tables, lovely children. And I watched three or
four year olds for ten minutes, and do you know what? Not once,
not once I tell you, not once during that ten minutes did one
child help another child. Each was doing something just for himself." But it would take relatively little effort and almost no expensive equipment to make cooperative play common practice in
the American school system.

As they grow older it becomes possible to involve children in
genuine responsibilities, to hold them accountable for these and
to give them scholastic credit as well as social approbation for
tasks well done. For instance, Urie Bronfenbrenner tells us how
the Russians have classes of older children take on responsibility
for the care of children of a lower grade level. A class of third
graders "adopts" a class of first graders in the same school or a
group attending a kindergarten in the immediate neighborhood.
The older children escort the younger ones to the school, play
with them on the playground, teach them new games, read to
them, help them to learn. All this is part of the regular curriculum and the children's performance is graded and credited as
such. Conceivably, this could be replicated here. Essentially the
same kind of experience could be provided for American children also by including, as core courses, instruction and experience
in family life and by locating day care centers and Head Start
programs either in schools or close enough by so that there would
be ample opportunities to learn by doing.

In the same vein, as children grow older and more knowledge-
able, there are many ways in which they can be given opportunities to participate as junior partners to adults in identifying
problems deserving of remedy at home, at school and in the community, and in helping to formulate and implement plans to
overcome them. This has the advantage, among other things, of
bringing children and adults closer together in mutually meaning-

ful ways. It also has the attribute of establishing the beginnings of personal autonomy. Autonomy, with its implications for decision-making, self-direction and self-responsibility, likewise can be cultivated at home by parents in numerous ways. For example, they can leave to the child the decision as to whether to spend his allowance, or earnings as the case might be, for some immediately gratifying experience, such as going to a show or a ballgame, or whether to save up for the bicycle for which he yearns. They can also grant to a child freedom to select his own hairstyle and, to a considerable extent, the kinds of clothes he wears.

*The arts.* As far back as the records of human endeavor reach, one finds evidences that man has expressed his innermost ideas and feelings through various forms of creative artistry. Even the simplest societies, which often were existing on a hand-to-mouth basis as far as essential life supports were concerned, allowed some of their members to expend a substantial amount of their energy in this manner. Hence our heritage of drawings in ancient caves and of art treasures hidden deep in tombs in Egyptian pyramids. The pyramids themselves are representative of human imagination inspired by an idea, concept or belief that went far beyond the simple representation of contemporary life realities.

These artistic products not only were profoundly meaningful to those who devised them — and more than a few have been willing practically to starve if necessary in order to satisfy their creative urge — but also have come to be among the most continuously treasured of all the things which men and women have ever produced from the beginning of their existence on earth. Even today, people travel great distances to visit the cathedrals of Europe, the temples of Asia, to see the Parthenon, to view the fine arts on display at the Louvre, in Florence, in the great American metropolitan art museums. They also throng to hear and see great artists perform masterpieces of music and dance. And many of the literary works written more than two thousand years ago are still numbered among the world's greatest.

These observations give evidence that artistic and literary works, architectural masterworks and other original forms of personal creativity are not just luxury items added on to life for their entertainment or pastime value when one cannot think of anything else to do. On the contrary, they probably come closest of all things to representing the core of those features which make human beings unique among all living things on earth.

The arts are becoming of increasing practical importance also, as opportunities to be successful through the production of goods or the procreation of hordes of children are being curtailed out of the necessity to maintain life on earth in a form that is worth experiencing, and they are being given close attention by contemporary urban designers. For example, in creating Harlow, one of the first of the new towns built a few miles outside London, England, the planners included a sizable arts center to provide residents with opportunities to learn how to be artistically creative and to perform or to display their products publicly. This is an important outlet in today's mechanized world. It has also had the additional value of giving children and adults something they can enjoy doing together.

*Sports and play.* Like the arts, sports have provided many people with opportunities to excel ever since the gladiators of Rome fought for glory and the amusement of the people. They have also served as a valuable, publicly acceptable outlet for man's desires to succeed competitively. Again, it is noteworthy that Harlow's designers also built a fine sports plaza, where family members can play games and test their skills. The attitude of the public toward these options is obvious in the fact that almost all Harlow residents who are able use regularly either the arts or sports facilities or both.

In our own country, one has only to walk for an hour or two through most slum and even many middle-class residential areas to discover that much too little attention has been given to providing our children and adults with these very healthy forms of outlet for their energies and ambitions.

We realize that though it would be great to have family sports and arts plazas in every American neighborhood, it is unlikely that doing so will be accomplished overnight. On the other hand, we can see no excuse for not including both the arts and the sports as basic parts of the school curriculum. We say this in the belief that our schools must become places where young people learn how to live successfully in the modern technological world and these healthy and enjoyable outlets play an important role in this.

*Concluding remarks.* Before we end this chapter we would like to focus attention once more on the role played by parents and others as the purveyors of these educational and socializing experiences to children. To begin with, it is clear that no pair of parents could possibly cover singlehandedly even a representative fraction of all the topics listed above. Society has recognized this by passing laws which require parents to hand their children over to the school system at about the age of six for a substantial portion of their upbringing.

In meeting the heavy demands placed upon it, the school system has grown to the point where it is now the single largest government enterprise. Even so, it has become evident that the schools cannot provide children with the training they need for a well-balanced life in modern America without the collaborative aid of museums, businesses, industry, government and public recreation resources. In other words, just about everybody has got to put his shoulder to this wheel to make it roll in the right direction and reach its destination.

In our schools, at an annual cost in excess of $90 billion, two million teachers are serving over fifty million pupils. This aspect of child-rearing in America has become heavily socialized, professionalized, monetized and bureaucratized. While potentially valuable on the one hand, this mammoth system is loaded with problems on the other. For one thing, it is difficult for parents to exert much influence upon the choice of subject matter or the ways and means by which it is exhibited to the pupils. For another, there is a natural tendency for many people, parents and teachers alike, to follow familiar pathways and to be reluctant to make innovative changes in scholastic curriculum — a topic concerning which we will have more to say in a subsequent chapter, "Education for Work." Consequently, school programs can become stultified, outmoded and uninteresting to a degree where children are bored and restless. Like the overpunishment that we were discussing in the beginning of this chapter, this dullness can result in negative attitudes toward schooling and learning, which can lead children to misbehave in the classroom and become such major management problems that teachers feel it necessary to function more as disciplinary officers than as instructors. Fortunately, it *is* possible to avoid and, when necessary, to overcome this type of difficulty. But this involves a considerable degree of renegotiation of the contract which parents as a group make with their school system as a social institution. In the final analysis, the manner and degree to which parents participate in the regulation of school affairs must be negotiated with the professionals, and we believe that the balance should be on the professional side. Otherwise, one is very likely to have a destructive situation, because most parents lack the expertise needed to be constructive rather than just disruptive. One way to avoid this type of situation is for the parents to gain a deeper understanding of the intricacies of modern childhood education through studying the subject with considerable care. Also, parents could be asked to participate in classes with their children or become involved in some other way in the running of the school day.

This raises questions as to who is responsible for what with regard to the goals of child-rearing and the ways and means by which they are to be reached. If parents have formed a mutually congenial personal attachment to their youngsters during their initial months and years, they will continue to play a significant role as the persons whose standards, approbation and criticisms are most meaningful to their children. On the other hand, if this attachment has not been formed early on, it becomes increasingly difficult for parents to develop and maintain a directive or guiding relationship with their children as they grow older.

The fact that most parents are not experts in education does not mean that they are impotent with regard to the educational system. Even those who are financially disadvantaged can be influential by joining with other parents in groups such as parent-teacher associations or by campaigning for school board candidates who stand for principles they espouse. Those who can afford to live in neighborhoods of their own choice or to send their children to private schools, summer camps or specialized teachers are in a stronger position. But, even in these cases, forces work upon their children which they cannot control as closely as parents could in the days when life was relatively un- complicated and people were living in close-knit, stable com- munities. Some of these forces, like TV and other mass media, are obvious. Others, such as ethical value systems underlying the policies and actions of government, industry and the advertising business may be hidden from sight yet profoundly influential for long periods of time. The same may be said of the influence which children may exert upon each other as peers.

What, then, can parents do under circumstances where chil- dren are being exposed to a multitude of different individuals whose orientation and activities range all the way from baby- sitting, day caretaking, preschooling, grammar-schooling, high- schooling, and summer camping to specialized tutors and coaches in sports, music, art, dancing, homemaking and so forth? To us, the fact that this list is so long and so diversified underlines the necessity for a continuing, overall primary generalist supervisor in the form of a parent who is interested and able to monitor, evaluate, balance and coordinate all these forces in ways which serve the best interests of the child. As with orchestra conductors and managers of other complex organizations, the individual must have enough familiarity with each of the various topics to which his children may be exposed, to be able to serve as a sympathetic and understanding sounding board as his children strive to pick and choose their way through this maze to programs which will best serve their developmental needs. This should be no great problem for those who have had a first-class general education during their own childhood. It may, however, be an insurmountably overwhelming task for those whose horizons have been severely limited by personal disadvantage.

This leads us back again to the question as to who is responsible for what as regards the goals and content of child-rearing in America today. In this particular instance, society has attempted to intervene once again in the parental role through providing children with guidance counselors as members of school staffs. Unfortunately, however, many people are not convinced our guidance counselors do much good.

There appear to be a number of reasons for this lack of confidence. For one thing, there are never enough guidance counselors. The public is presented with them in a school budget as "auxiliary, nonteaching personnel," so, understandably, the public assumes that they are "frills" and an unnecessary drain on the taxpayers' money. For another, many counselors lack dependable ways and means for predicting the areas of endeavor in which a given individual is likely to function successfully. For still another, most have very little information to use when they try to anticipate in what areas there is likely to be a substantial demand for workers. This aspect of their problem could be eased, we believe, by developing and publishing, at least annually, a national roster of currently filled job slots with estimates of potential job openings during the next year, based on help wanted and anticipated age-related obligatory retirement statistics. To be maximally useful, these statistics on potential jobs should include listings of all the personal service as well as production roles based on a broadly representative inquiry of publicly felt needs. It is likely that in due course trends would become evident which would enable experts to project job opportunities further and further into the future, just as the United States Weather Bureau has been doing recently with weather trends. It is encouraging to learn that the Manpower Institute of Washington, D.C., is striving to develop just this type of public resource.

There remains always the interesting fact that one will never be able to predict precisely what the demand will be for work roles which have never existed before. For instance, the moon shot created a need for thousands of superspecialized workers for a few years. Though that job is now completed, one can be sure that there will be other totally new opportunities for those having a high degree of competence to deal effectively with complex problems — be they technical, mechanical, political, economic, social or whatever.

It is important to cultivate in young people a capacity for

adaptation to changing circumstances, which should be based on a generously broad knowledge of the basics of natural and social phenomena capped with specialized skills in a few areas of particular *interest* to the individual. Viewed against this background, it could well be that the role of the so-called "counselor" would become more valuable if he could serve effectively as a channel through which youth could both obtain information about job market prospects and requirements and gain opportunities to test out potential interests in various fields while there is still time to cultivate areas which appeal to him and are reasonably promising as jobs. It is probably unrealistic to aim for more help for children on a personal level from guidance counselors because there just aren't enough of them to enable them really to know the students they advise. But they could bring much creativity and inspiration to the job of searching out avenues for children to follow. We will have more to say about this topic in Chapter 7 when we are focusing on "Education for Work."

# 6

## TV—Good or Bad?

WHEN the first image was transmitted without wires in 1927, something very new and powerful was added to the dimensions of life in the modern world. Today, about 96 percent of the total United States population has television sets. They are more commonplace than telephones, bathtubs, toasters, vacuum cleaners and even the daily newspaper. This is true even among families having incomes below three thousand dollars, 90 percent of whom have at least one set. Consequently, TV is as much and more a basic fact of life for American children as the stove their food is cooked on, the table they sit to eat at, the bed they sleep on.

Unlike these relatively inanimate objects, television has a special kind of vitality which, like the mythical sirens of old, can attract and hold people spellbound for hours at a time. Nowhere is this more clearly evident than among preschool children, who nowadays are spending about fifty-four hours a week in the fall and forty-six hours a week in the spring viewing television. By the time they reach high school, they have spent on the average twelve thousand hours in school and fifteen thousand hours watching television. This is the equivalent of spending two full years, twenty-four hours a day, sitting in front of the television screen. The only thing they spend more time doing is sleeping. One of the effects of this television watching has been to reduce substantially the amount of time children spend being physically active.

Even without delving deeply, one can sense that TV as a mass medium also may be exerting a powerful influence upon the ways children perceive the world and the way people think and act.

As one parent remarked, TV has the power to hold children motionless, slack-jawed, eyes unblinking, while they drink in the sights and sounds coming from the television apparatus, meanwhile working furiously to organize their perception of this new experience. Parents often use television as a mechanical entertainer, an alternate to a human babysitter. This form of babysitting may be having a significant effect upon children starting very early in life, as can be seen in the frequent reports of children whose first words are "Budweiser" or "Clairol," or who learned to spell Mickey Mouse before they could spell their own names. Any agent capable of producing these responses is certainly worthy of close scrutiny and appraisal as a potentially major force for good or evil in the lives of its viewers.

We can start with the very elementary observation that TV is a window on the world for those who live in remote areas where one could spend a lifetime never having seen a mountain, or the sea, or a zoo, or a fire station, or a ballet or a work of art. Now, in watching TV eight hours a day, as many children do, they become visually and aurally aware of the existence of these and endless numbers of other worldly realities. Often these are presented as they exist or are happening at the moment, transporting the mind of the viewer to the place where the camera is almost as if he had been transported there bodily. Thus, TV has made the world a global village and everyone a citizen of the whole as well as of the particular place in which they happen to be living.

Television was not generated primarily for the edification of children or adults. Rather it was and still is used largely for purposes of commercial profit, political aggrandizement and other similarly mundane concerns. This use was presaged by the fact that Farlow T. Farnsworth used the dollar sign as the test pattern when he transmitted the first television image in 1927. To a considerable extent such use has been necessary because the costs of putting shows on the air run as high as $100,000 per hour, and even higher if animated cartoons are included. It is also understandable because TV advertising has proven to be a very lucrative business. On the other hand, it has had some unhappy consequences as far as children are concerned. These have stemmed from the fact that advertisers discovered that shows directed at children under eleven years of age comprise an effective means for selling toys, candies and other goods. As far as commercial television advertisers are concerned, all who are over eleven years old are considered to be "adults." According to recent estimates, the average "child" watches 22,000 to 25,000 TV commercials a year!

One of the unfortunate aspects of this watching is that many of the items being pushed in these advertisements are *not* good for children. For example, until a year or so ago one company set out to sell via children's TV ads a product which was dispensed in bottles which carried on the label the warning "Keep out of reach of children!" This sales pitch was halted only after a group called "Action For Children's Television" brought it to the attention of the public at large. The product was a vitamin pill. Sugary foods and soft drinks that predispose to dental caries and to imbalanced diets likewise have been extensively promoted. Moreover, toys are being sold to children which are the worst toys that the industry makes — worst in the sense that they are poorly made or downright dangerous because of sharp edges and points, brittle plastic or glass that can be broken easily, small parts that can get loose and wind up lodged in a child's windpipe, guns that make so much noise that they may deafen the ears, and so on. Many of these have now been banned from the market by our government.

Our point is simply that in too many instances the manufacturers and advertisers did not take it upon themselves in the interest of the welfare of children to see to it that only products that are safe for young people are made in the first place, and advertised in the second. This is just another down-to-earth example of how business and industry are in many ways playing a consequential role in creating appetites, setting standards, and thereby either protecting or hurting children. While there is a paucity of direct observations on the manner in which these advertisements affect children directly, there is compelling indirect evidence that this kind of advertising can be very persuasive. For instance, one toy firm grew in two years from a $500,000 a year to an $8,000,000 a year company by selling to children mostly on Saturday morning TV shows. And they were just one of the many who have been investing about $400 million a year in advertising directed to children. Of this about $75 million are spent just on Saturday morning alone. In view of all this, one also wonders whether the extensive use of violence in commercial shows aimed at capturing children's attention may not be having more profound effects than we are willing to acknowledge. Even though we do not know for sure, it seems highly unlikely that heavy exposure to scenes of violence and unethical behavior and to thousands upon thousands of human death scenes can be without influence upon the value systems which our children and youth are building within themselves as they grow up in America today.

One is tempted to believe that in a capitalistic society such as ours, profiteering forces of this magnitude are so far beyond our control as individual citizens that we are rendered powerless to do anything about them. We know of no more encouraging evidence to the contrary than that provided by "Action For Children's Television" (called ACT for short), mentioned above. This was founded in 1969 by a group of parents and professional people concerned with child development who believed that it should be possible to improve situations of this sort. Their goals as a nonprofit, nonpolitical, national group, are to enlighten parents and others involved with children about the importance of television's effects on children; to persuade broadcasters and advertisers to provide high-quality programs designed to meet the needs of children at various stages of their development; to eliminate commercialism from children's programs, substituting for this a new system of support based on underwriting and public service funding.

ACT now has about five thousand dues-paying members scattered across the United States. The influence of this membership is enhanced by collaborative working arrangements with other major national organizations concerned with the welfare of children.

ACT works to change the climate of decision-making regarding children's TV through a variety of means. One has been to stimulate the Federal Communications Commission to hold inquiries into children's TV; the public's response was the largest the Commission has ever experienced – they received over one hundred thousand communications, which filled sixty-five volumes with letters and comments. The second approach has been by petitioning the Federal Trade Commission and the Federal Communications Commission to eliminate TV advertising directed toward children. A third has been by testifying at congressional hearings, and another was producing a film called "But First This Message," which shows the kind of material with which network TV has been bombarding children. Their impact is reflected in a recent decision of the National Association of Broadcasters to change their code, thereby reducing the time allowed for children's advertising by 40 percent. This change was subsequently endorsed by the Federal Communications Commission, which indicated to the broadcasters that they should make a continued strong commitment to meeting the needs of children in their programming.

This effort has double significance. It not only has accomplished something specific on behalf of children's TV experiences, but it also has demonstrated that a group of lay citizens, working mostly as a grass roots organization, *can* exert a powerful influence on matters pertaining to child well-being by directing well-organized efforts at the right places. We believe that this model could be applied advantageously to overcome many of the other shortcomings which we have encountered in the course of the explorations already set forth in this book.

Starting back in the early 1950's, efforts were being made to develop programs designed specifically to foster the development of children. The first of these, "Captain Kangaroo," was produced by the Columbia Broadcasting System. It was, and still is, concerned with instilling cultural values in preschool children. In the early 1960's, the National Broadcasting Company asked producer Craig Fisher to develop "Exploring" as a high-quality weekly program. Fisher in turn asked Professor Gerald S. Lesser of Harvard University to put his expertise in the fields of education and psychology to work to find out what could be done to improve the program as the series progressed. He did so by observing children as they watched the show and studying their reactions to it. This marked the beginning of a significant effort to take advantage of the unique opportunities provided by TV to explore systematically some fundamental aspects of childhood teaching and learning. For example, what kinds of experience hold children's attention; what do they learn from these and what do they fail to learn, and in each instance, why and how. These are the kinds of question which, when answered accurately and viewed without prejudice, have formed the basis for many of the major gains in child care realized over recent decades.

Another milestone was laid in 1968 when Joan Ganz Cooney, together with Lloyd Morrisett of the Carnegie Institute and Gerald Lesser, formed the Children's Television Workshop. Their first product, "Sesame Street," went on the air via the noncommercial, nonprofit public television system in 1969. It was started with the premise that many three- four- and five-year-old youngsters don't have organized educational experiences available to them. Their aim was to provide these children with supplementary audiovisual experiences which would help make them more ready to enter kindergarten and first grade and to adapt to their early schooling comfortably and rapidly. In this series they have focused on the cultivation of language skills, number skills, reasoning and problem solving.

The "Sesame Street" programs have been produced ever since at the rate of one hundred thirty one-hour shows a year. As they went along, the producers sought answers to the questions: has this program been of significant value to the viewers and does having learned the things we portray make a difference to the way these children perform when they get to school? The teacher's responses have been affirmative — most find that these youngsters are better prepared and readier for school. Parents also like and approve the show. In a three-city survey, in which mothers were asked if viewing "Sesame Street" during preschool years made any difference in the development of their children who are now in school, 90 percent of those residing in New York

City, 89 percent of those living in Chicago and 84 percent of those from Washington, D.C., replied affirmatively. Specifically, they said that the programs taught their children how to count, helped them to learn the alphabet and aided them in their reading ability. The mothers of Spanish-speaking children said also that it helped their children learn to speak English.

Two years later, in 1971, Children's Television Workshop inaugurated a second series, "The Electric Company." This time their specific objective was to teach reading to second-, third- and fourth-grade pupils who were having difficulty learning how to read. In a deliberate effort to collect data concerning the effectiveness of their program, they learned that those who had viewed their programs during school hours had made greater gains in regard to every one of the skills they had set out to teach than did those who had not seen the TV material in school. This gain was in addition to the gains ordinarily achieved in school. So far it appears that this program accomplished three things simultaneously: it transmitted basic reading skills to the children; it alleviated the personal suffering which comes when one is not able to keep up with one's peers, and it advanced the viewer's knowledge beyond that ordinarily acquired at this stage of schooling.

Another pioneering effort in public television broadcasting was launched in 1972 under the title "Zoom" by Channel 2, WGBH, in Boston. Targeted at eight- to twelve-year-old children, the program is designed to stimulate children to be creative and to participate. Its objective is attuned to the fact that this is the period in children's lives when they begin to leave home and test out their ideas on their peers. In pursuing this objective, its originator, Christopher Sarson, had the idea that TV could and should be more than something you just sit and watch. It should be something that stimulates you to do things that you might not do otherwise and provides you with opportunities to develop a sense of belonging by participating with others.

The show itself is organized and performed by children in the eight- to twelve-year-old age group, with the help and guidance of adult professional broadcasters. The ideas that they portray come from contemporaries who have observed previous TV programs. They are regularly invited by the child performers to mail in their ideas. The children are told, "Come on, give it a try. Send us your ideas. We *care* about your ideas and this is where they will be heard."

In the first year alone over five hundred and ninety thousand letters were received. At least half of these carried creative ideas — something the child had picked up while viewing the show, taken unto himself, developed into an original thought and sent back to the program. It is estimated that each of these children probably spent on the average about an hour in finding a pencil and paper, writing and sending his or her message to "Zoom." Adding all this up, one comes to the impressive estimate that somewhere between six and seven "child years" of personal effort was expended in writing these letters. It is also worth noting that one of the goals of "Zoom" has been to reach disadvantaged children. Accordingly, "Zoom" uses only tools and materials which are readily available to children who have limited resources.

The following quotes from remarks made by parents who have viewed some of the "Zoom" programs may give those of our readers who have not had an opportunity to see it some ideas of what these shows are like and what kind of impact they have on their child audiences. For example, one parent stated, "The show absolutely rivets kids in their chairs — they just love it." It also gets them out of their chairs in search of what they need to duplicate the action they have seen. For example, "there is a kid who builds a raft and that is the whole thing. He is just there, and he starts from scratch. You come in on an open field. There is some brushwood on the ground and you wonder what the heck the kid is going to do. Then he begins to build a raft, and six minutes later he is floating down the river on his raft. And you have seen him do it and the kids of the TV audience have kibitzed the whole operation. The next thing you know, those kids who have been watching go out and try to do likewise."

What makes "Zoom" programming work so well is that the performers aren't stars, they are not the Mouseketeers, the Brady Bunch or the Partridge Family. They are just kids like the viewers themselves. The result is that the viewers identify as closely with the "Zoom" cast of children as some adults do with members of their favorite ball teams.

The impact of these programs may be illustrated by quoting a dialogue between two adults who were for a period at a loss to understand why certain program sequences which they found dull were so fascinating to their children. Said one, "I had a chance to observe some children as they were watching one of the first shows. One of the things that seemed to go on forever was a bunch of kids playing jacks. There were jacks spread out on the floor and here they were playing with them. I couldn't understand why these children were as fascinated as they seemed to be. We had a chance to talk with them a little bit afterwards about what had held their attention and what hadn't. When we got to that issue, it became very clear what held them. It was not only the jack game, which they found interesting in its own right, but it was the fact that a little boy was playing with a couple of girls and beating them. They were playing a girls' game and what the kids were watching was the little boy wiping out the little girls."

"My daughter watched the same show," said another observer, "and she insisted I get her some jacks. Well, I went to get them, the Five and Dime was out of them. So was every other store in the shopping center. Jacks had been out of style for a long while, but when the kids watched that program they went out and bought them like crazy. That happens in relation to everything that takes place on that show."

"Zoom" is typical of many of the finest American public television programs in that the show operates for public benefit rather than for profit. Accordingly, it is dependent upon grants and gifts from the government, industry and individuals.

"Zoom" came close to having to close down in 1973 when the Corporation for Public Broadcasting failed to renew its grant. In response to a "Zoom-Alarm," thousands of drawings by children poured in to the broadcasting station, WGBH, with letters and telegrams from both children and adults urging the CPB to reconsider its decision. As a result, CPB agreed to fund half of the

"Zoom" budget for the ensuing year in the amount of $565,000. A short time later, McDonald's Corporation announced it would underwrite the other half. As of June 1975, the funding for "Zoom" is once again so uncertain that there is a real risk that the program will have to be discontinued within a month. It is hoped that this problem will have been solved by the time this book is published. If so, it will be an example of the conversion of public concern into explicit public support. If not, we hope that through wider realization of the value of this type of television to American children the resources needed for the support of this type of constructive effort can be marshaled.

Over and above the primary accomplishments outlined above, TV has provided valuable opportunities to sharpen our appreciation of factors which may be essential to successful teaching and learning. One cannot accomplish anything along these lines without first getting and holding the attention of one's pupil. There are only a few ways in which this can be done successfully. One is by entertaining; another by causing the individual to think that what one is saying is of vital importance to him; and a third is by stimulating a desire to get in, to contribute, to be creative, to be part of some activity. About the only other reason why anyone should want to pay attention to another is because of friendship.

In this context, the word *entertaining* means presenting something in a way that children find enjoyable because it provides them with information which is new and interesting, that causes them to laugh from time to time, that allows them to get up and move around occasionally and that treats them kindly and does not threaten them in punitive ways. This is in contradistinction to situations where parents or teachers are pressing children to "learn" or to do things in conformity with parental or cultural norms under threat of disparagement or punishment if they fail to live up to expectations. Far beyound the predictions of many, properly applied teaching mixed with entertainment can hold the attention even of three-year-olds for as long as an hour.

For something to be of vital importance to a pupil, and hence readily teachable, circumstances must be conducive. We all can remember the times we have been stimulated to learn to the utmost limits of our capacity when we had an examination of crucial importance to our future career coming up. But there are many other more natural reasons for wanting to learn. To take a commonplace example, it might be that a child is keenly desirous to learn how to ride his bicycle in order that he can keep up with his pals. Or it could be that one simply wants to earn the acceptance and approbation of one's parents or one's peers by acquiring knowledge and skills they consider valuable.

Receptivity to learning can be enhanced further by current events. For example, when Martin Luther King was assassinated, a crash program was undertaken by station WGBH of Boston to get a documentary about urban race relations on the air for high school students. Teachers were worried that this was going to be too rough for these young people to take. But it turned out that they were very concerned about the problems the country was facing as a result of the race riots. Consequently, they were, as David Ives, president of WGBH, put it, "warm and receptive to receive the message." He added that there was nothing entertaining about this show. It was, in fact, horrifying. But it really did get to them.

As far as participation is concerned, we have described how one can hook eight-to twelve-year-old children by a program like "Zoom" in which children invite other children to participate and give evidence of caring about each one individually, of respecting their ideas and so forth. In instances where children get little or no sense of personal value from their own family, such corporate expressions of interest and valuation can be enormously helpful as supplementary, although vicarious, sources of these essential social supplies.

Another thing that makes television constructive for children is the fact that people like Samuel Gibbon, one of the original programmers of "Sesame Street," have taken advantage of the capacity of this medium to generate presentations which enable children to predict reality more accurately. The same may be said of the programmers' ability to represent to children processes, ideas and connections between things that have been talked about, but never shown before. Pictures of the earth taken from the moon serve as one familiar example, and there are countless others.

In contrast to most of the foregoing, there has been a good deal of reluctance to use TV as a medium for transmitting messages about affective issues such as "Should programs like 'Sesame Street' teach children to trust strangers?" The trouble is that no one is sure of the answer, because the answer is not the same under all circumstances. For example, it could be good for children in a safe, middle-class neighborhood, but might not be at all good for children living in a crime-ridden ghetto area. However, there do appear to be a few universals concerning which almost everyone is in agreement. One is that when you are faced with a task, you should not be afraid of failing — you should face frustration or failure without collapsing.

Probably the nearest thing to a major program on this topic to date has been Fred Rogers's "Mr. Rogers' Neighborhood" program. The program was inaugurated in 1967. By the time it closes down in June of 1975, Rogers will have taped five hundred shows at WQED, Pittsburgh's public television station, in association with Pittsburgh's Child Study Center. Concentrating on the emotional problems of preschool youngsters, the center found that children use these programs for about two to two and a half years and then grow out of them, just as they outgrow books such as *The Wizard of Oz*. The important thing here is that it probably will be possible in due course to use the television medium successfully and appropriately for transmitting concepts about value systems, such as honesty versus dishonesty and fair versus foul play, without having the show backfire or otherwise fall flat on its face. So even though this is an area which may be loaded with booby traps and boomerangs, it is one which can and should be cautiously approached, if for no other reason than that standards and values are of decisive importance to everyone's way of life.

Responsible parents and their surrogates have at their fingertips the option to monitor TV shows and to turn the switch off when they consider them to be either injurious or just a terrible waste of time. Furthermore and most important, they can influence what is being programmed by backing up the experts in child development who are working with the nation's public TV stations to promote constructive TV material for children. They can also join in making a serious effort to convince commercial houses that it will pay off for them to contribute their fair share by investing in American youth instead of exploiting them for profit.

As we reflect on all the issues raised in the course of this chapter, we have come to the conclusion that television as a mass medium has become an enormously powerful force in the socialization of children. Like everything else of any importance, it has within it both formative and destructive capabilities. We know of no better way to get the "bad" out than by working hard to put more that is "good" in.

# 7

## Education for Work

FROM the beginning of human history, there has been a tendency for some to consider work to be a necessary but unfortunate component of life, and to view leisure as a more desirable mode of existence. In earlier times, the rich and powerful have been able, if they wished, to live a life of ease by enslaving others or by hiring servants to do their work for them. Now, as human slavery and servitude have waned, we have been able to accomplish by means of automatic machines many of the tasks which people would otherwise have to do by hand. So, still today, many of us know the taste of free hours gained vicariously by harnessing inanimate forms of energy to serve our purposes.

While we relish a modicum of leisure as much as anyone, we hold to the position that work is an absolutely essential component of satisfactory living.

We would like to spend a moment now embellishing this concept by quoting some of the thoughts expressed by seminar participants during the course of our meetings. Considering the nature of work, Willard Wirtz observed, "Our whole experience has been one of thinking not about work, but about labor as an element of production. We don't get near where we want to go until we recognize also that work is an essential human value. The function of both education and work is to maximize the opportunity for every individual to make the highest and best use of the human experience." Speaking along parallel lines, Charles Sanders declared, "I feel the greatest human satisfaction one can have is to accomplish something which requires work. We work because that gives man significance in his own eyes. By substituting machines for men, our technology is seriously hurting our ability to achieve this goal because leisure should not be the end goal for any man or woman's being. Yet our whole political system is geared toward how you can have more leisure and do less work. How do we realize the beauty of humanity — which is accomplishment — without a political system which promotes this particular goal?" In the same vein, Sheldon White remarked, "I find myself thinking there is something existential about the need for work. I guess people feel that if they don't have work, they're really, in a funny way, socially dead."

But for work to have this positive value to people, it must have certain characteristics. For example, work to those living in slavery probably was not very soul-satisfying. Even today, some are living under circumstances where they may be feeling somewhat the same dissatisfactions. Speaking to this problem, Phyllis Wallace noted, "Black teenage girls have a very negative perception of the world of work. This is because, in low-income black families, the adults have experienced not only a lot of unemployment and difficulty in finding jobs, but also a lot of concentration in unskilled jobs and jobs that didn't pay very much." So, as Mary Rowe observed, work should be defined "as an occupation which does not damage or downgrade, which uses skills and provides a chance to acquire others, which enhances other life roles, which provides for good work group relations, and which produces goods and services that make us feel that we have accomplished something valuable."

In the same vein, Jerome Kagan deems, "Our problem in America is somehow to define work so that it does not mean only salary, but also effort for community benefit and for self-actualization. We have to be much more imaginative and think of ways which will allow an individual to use his skills, whatever they are, to permit him to feel he is contributing creatively toward a good that transcends him, whether there is a paycheck or not." In line with this, Charles Sanders thinks that it is "our responsibility to provide employment opportunities through which kids can find out that there really is something to be gained by going to work and accomplishing something and deriving satisfaction from that."

This stance brings to the fore as a problem the fact that much of the work which is now being done by adults is not such as to elevate this sense of self-worth other than by giving them the feeling that they are earning their keep. This is particularly true of the depersonalized jobs, in which humans are functioning almost mechanically, like robots, doing routine or repetitive tasks. This situation leads us to make a plea for more governmental support of human service opportunities like child care, senior citizen care, volunteer hospital aid, recreation activities, home-helping efforts and so forth. These are activities which have low priority today, but from the human point of view, they are exceedingly important both to those who perform them and those who benefit from them. Moreover, they are activities which children and adults can do together.

The same is true of a wide variety of individually performed handicrafts which likewise can yield both valuable products and a sense of personal accomplishment. At the industrial level, too, many socially concerned individuals are exploring ways and means for devising conditions which are more compatible with a humanly satisfying work life.

Renato Tagiuri has drawn up a set of criteria for judging the quality of work-life arrangements which provide us with guidelines which are both practicable and thought-provoking. They are paraphrased below; it is held that workers should:

(1) receive adequate and fair compensation;

(2) have safe and healthy working conditions;

(3) have immediate opportunities to use and develop their human capacities (specifically, they should have some degree of autonomy; should have the opportunity to develop multiple skills and to apply those from time to time; thereby gaining variety in life; should have a perception of the role they are playing in relation to the total work process; should have some opportunities to complete whole tasks and should be able to do a little of the planning);

(*4*) be given opportunities for continual personal growth through learning and developing new abilities, thereby gaining increased flexibility and security;

(*5*) be integrated into the work organization by membership in face-to-face groups which have some meaning, in which everyone knows each other and through which one relates openly with co-members of the work community both horizontally at one's own level and vertically with those of higher and lower rank (it was with a view to accomplishing these kinds of relationships that the Volvo company changed their automobile manufacturing procedure from an assembly line set-up to a factory shaped like a clover leaf, where in small areas the workers gained a sense of being members of a little shop);

(*6*) be provided contractually in the work organization with the right to privacy, to free speech and equity through "due process";

(*7*) be able to work in ways relative to their total life situation such that they need not sacrifice their families or give up all normal private leisure and recreational activities or have to uproot and transplant their homes "once every five years" as has been the "norm" in America in recent years;

(*8*) be able to see the relevance of their work to the needs of the larger society — to perceive that the organization they are working for is socially responsible in terms of current values.

Against this background set of ideals, it is interesting to take a look at what American youth are getting today in the way of preparation for work and work experiences and rewarding job opportunities.

We can gain some perspective regarding the realities of the current American work world by reviewing some of the data which have been compiled by the United States Department of Labor. As of a year or so ago, about 86 million of our citizens were employed in civilian jobs. Nine of ten were white, one was nonwhite. Ninety-one of every hundred were adults and nine were teenagers. Of these, slightly more than half were boys. About 48 percent of all workers were white-collar, 35 were blue-collar, 13 were in service and 4 were working on farms. This last figure is of special interest because it reflects the fact that the family farms, businesses and cottage industries in which sons and daughters could participate as apprentices and future partners have almost disappeared. Most of the jobs now available to teen-agers during their school years are "dead-end" in nature; most employers in this country are not interested in hiring on a con-tinuing basis anyone who is still in school and/or is under twenty years of age with the thought that the individual will grow up in the business. Nevertheless, as of a year ago, over four million sixteen- to nineteen-year-olds were doing paid work of some sort while still in school. Moreover, they had obtained these jobs essentially by dint of their own efforts, without institutional help.

Continuing with our categories of work, we know further that 30 percent of the white-collar workers are functioning at profes-sional and technical levels, 35 percent hold clerical jobs, 20 per-cent hold managerial and administrative posts and 15 percent are sales people. Of the blue-collar workers, 35 of every one hun-dred are craftsmen or foremen, 50 are in production and 15 are laborers. If we assume that education beyond high school to the level of college-granted bachelor's degree is necessary for most managerial and high-level administrative posts, and that master's or doctoral degrees are a requisite for all professional and so-phisticated technical jobs, it would appear that education much beyond high school is really necessary only for approximately one quarter of all the jobs slots available today.

This estimate accords with the findings of the Carnegie Com-mission on Higher Education, which concluded in its report on college graduates and jobs that only about 20 percent of the jobs in the United States require more than a high school education. At the same time, the report also indicates that about 60 percent of those presently seeking work have had at least some college experience. What this means is that while the percentage of people who attend college and the number who graduate is rising sharply, the percentage of jobs that require college education is not keeping pace. Substantial numbers of young people are being grossly overtrained for the available jobs and undertrained in the practical kinds of skills they will need for the job slots that will actually need to be filled. For example, current reports indicate that in the 1970's we are training about four million teachers for two million prospective teaching posts. The implications of this for those who find themselves in the predicament of being overtrained in relation to the requirements of the marketplace are now being reflected in news articles appearing under such titles as "Can a Ph.D. Find Happiness as a Necktie Salesman?"

Recent national labor data indicate that at least 16 percent of American youth in the sixteen-to nineteen-year age group are unemployed — a fantastic figure inasmuch as this is more than four times the unemployment rate for our population as a whole, and the indications are that they have not peaked out yet.* Over one-third of what we call unemployment in the United States occurs in this age group. If the age group is extended to twenty-four years, we discover that half the unemployment in this country is to be found among these young people; the same is now true in other technologically advanced countries. Unemployment statistics, which have been kept for nearly thirty years, show that youth unemployment has always been higher than adult unemployment, but that it has worsened seriously during the past twenty years. Moreover, it has risen even as economic activity reached all-time heights, which is a trend opposite to the usual. Considering the rapid increase in the proportion of teenagers in the population during these years, it is surprising that youth unemployment has not risen even higher.

Taking these data at face value may be misleading. To paraphrase Cervantes, "Facts are enemies to the truth," because the figures tell too little and also say too much. In this case they tell too little because the 16 percent figure does not reflect differences in unemployment in different youth populations. Among those who are young and black, the unemployment figure is more than 30 percent. A recent study by Phyllis Wallace shows that the number rises even higher for black girls sixteen to nineteen years of age who are out of school and live in urban-poverty neighborhoods. These young women have the highest rates of

* These unemployment rates have risen substantially since this text was prepared in mid-1975.

unemployment of anybody in the American labor market — between 40 and 50 percent. When they venture out in search of jobs, they find that they are always placed at the end of the queue. Everywhere they go they are told, "We have to help welfare mothers, or males, or veterans or somebody else, but not you." As a result, many develop an intensely negative picture of themselves. This reinforces the negative impression of the world of work already generated in them by their parents, who have experienced this same problem for many years. It also underscores a high need for the "affirmative action" which our government is currently requiring — that is, that employers with government contracts make an explicit effort to search out minority-group as well as non-minority-group candidates for staff positions and consider them strictly in relation to their capacity to fill the role irrespective of sex, race and social class standing. "Affirmative action" does not, alas, cover firms that have no government contracts. However, there are some antidiscrimination laws that do.

At the opposite end of the scale, the 16 percent youth unemployment figure is misleading because it includes young people who are looking for work but are also in school. Their "part-time unemployment" has different implications from the full-time unemployment of older men and women who have families dependent upon them for support.

A third weakness of the unemployment data is that they fail to reflect the fact that many young people who are not officially classified as unemployed would prefer to be working, but remain in school because they think that jobs are not available to them. Particularly for such older children, school may be nothing more than a vast parking lot. This is extraordinarily wasteful of human capabilities.

We will have more to say about the availability of jobs for youth later on in this chapter. Meanwhile, we would like to spend a few moments thinking about the ways in which parents and schools can, and perhaps should, be striving to help the young people make the transition from childhood to adolescence to adult life. The key to this is the development of roles which enable the young to participate in productive adult activities and to assume increasing degrees of real responsibility for what they do. There is no shortage of possibilities since there are about forty thousand different vocations in the American dictionary of occupations. Up to this time, the shortages have resulted more from the obstacles placed in the way of youthful participation as a result of the reduction and, in many cases, elimination of home chores, legal limitations placed on youth employment, minimum wage requirements, sophisticated specialization and so on. But these obstacles are more apparent than real.

Even during the child's earliest years, parents can encourage natural inclinations to learn how to master a range of materials. For example, in one family we know, when Jimmy was four, it was evident to his parents that he was happiest when disassembling motors. So for birthday and Christmas gifts they canvassed junkyards and service stations for old carburetors and other mechanical parts. By the time he was six, Jimmy had helped his father install the basic electrical wiring and the burglar alarm system — ready to be hooked up by a licensed electrician — and all the insulation in the new family home. Then they built furniture. Soon he was as competent in the use of safe tools, like hammers and bow saws, as his parents. By the time he was ten, he had learned many of the basic mechanical skills that he would need as an auto mechanic, a pilot, a surgeon or a jeweler, to mention just a few examples.

Similarly, one of his sisters at the age of seven, taught herself to sew. Bored one day, she asked her mother for some spare cloth and inquired how one makes a dolly. All her mother told her was to draw it first on paper and then cut it out. The Little Green Man she created became the prototype of many delightful dolls she made for other children. The other sister taught herself weaving and pottery work. All three of the children have helped to grow and can hundreds of dollars' worth of food. By the time these children are eighteen, they should be able to support themselves in any one of many practical ways — farming, craftswork, mechanical work. Although the interest and support of these parents and their availability as models were significant factors, the most important thing that they did was to make available to children what they needed and to leave them to their own devices.

Children who have parents who can respond to their needs for creative outlets are fortunate indeed. But a lot of families in disadvantaged areas have no place, no tools and no materials available; and a lot of children in both disadvantaged and affluent homes have parents who are too lacking in ideas and skills or too preoccupied with personal problems to give their children the support they need to blossom in this way. Children need multiple skills, and they need self-confidence — the feeling that they can master their environment. This is where schools can become extremely valuable as alternative or additional sources of opportunities to learn the elements of skillful, creative workmanship. Some good child care centers do this at early ages, but few elementary schools do it. Part of the problem is that most teachers are not being trained, paid well enough and provided with the resources needed to do this kind of work. This doesn't have to be true. Within schools, children can be provided with opportunities to learn how to do many of the things that they will be doing as adults. If more of this is done, more avenues opened to children in schools — and we mean carpentry for girls too; cooking, sewing, design for boys — we might find that many young people will discover unique and more self-satisfying vocations for themselves than the college and graduate school route they might otherwise have taken — only to find in the end no job openings and unhappiness and frustration.

George Richmond speaks compellingly about this subject. For one thing, he feels that the great social issues of the day are being submerged as a result of being preoccupied with efforts to get students through school to college, or to keep bored, restless students under disciplinary control. As we know, the latter problem has made more than a few junior high and high schools combat zones where the struggle between teachers and students is so unpleasant that it is intensifying alienation and minimizing the chances that anything educationally valuable can be transmitted.

As an alternative, he has been developing and testing out in schools the concept that such anachronistic efforts need not dominate the learning scene. Out of this evolved the idea that it might be constructive to direct the energies which children and their teachers have been expending in classroom wars to solving, on a miniscale, some of the problems that every responsible person faces in the course of his or her daily life. Out of this have evolved "microsociety" classrooms, in which students simulate many of the economic, political, legal and ethical components of life in modern society.

For instance, students and their teachers have developed and operated newspapers, savings banks, a commercial bank, a variety of crafts enterprises, commercial "streets" teeming with small businesses, comic-book publishing, theaters, clothes dyeing outfits, a post office, tutorial programs, math game businesses, a greeting card company and so on. For older students, the aim has been to help and encourage them to explore and gain primary experience in accounting, business, engineering, city planning, architecture, law, medicine and almost any other profession, in accordance with their individual tastes and talents. These students also have tackled many questions representative of the salient political, legal and ethical issues. As a representative, "should I vote from my conscience or do I have to obey the will of the people who elected me?" This was just one of the many questions raised in the course of several months in a "constitutional convention" designed to define the politics of their microsociety.

The breadth and depth of this type of schooling is further enhanced by the presentation and discussion of such questions as: "How do the rich get rich?" "Are you poor?" "Do we create welfare for children in this class who don't have enough money?" "Should we tax you to pay for it?" "How should we deal with someone who steals someone else's money?" "How rich should the rich get?" As one person observed, tackling topics of this sort, well-backed with information represented in the humanities, social .sciences, natural sciences and with access to experts in business, law or government and so forth, makes schooling dangerously close to being interesting for all concerned!

In response to an awareness of the need for new roles for teenagers in the school and the community, the National Commission on Resources for Youth was founded in 1967 as a spontaneous action by a group of educators, social scientists, judges and businessmen who had been concerned with the well-being of youth. Working under the direction of Judge Mary Conway Kohler, they began their work by investigating promising programs from communities all over the nation which had been brought to their attention. They appraised them carefully, weeding out those of doubtful value and retaining those which provided for wholehearted, responsible participation of youth and which were feasible for widespread adoption. Members of the commission are convinced that projects of the kinds they are now endorsing demonstrate clearly that youths can be tremendous assets to society rather than burdens. They also point out that we have many institutions in the United States which provide important public services — day care centers, old age homes, museums, mental hospitals, transportation services — but are unable to keep up with the demands made on them partly because they lack adequate numbers of competent, dedicated people working in them. The commission's published report states: "At the national level, VISTA and the Teachers Corps are two examples of response to this challenge. At the local level, programs for developing the potentialities of volunteer manpower have proliferated and, increasingly, these programs are focusing on what is probably the largest, the most zestful and the most under-used manpower pool of all — the nation's youth."

Training is essential to the performance of these service tasks and to deriving satisfaction from doing them. One ideal way to accomplish this is by including community service, with scholastic credit for work well done, within the overall educational program offered at school. The areas in which great successes have been had already are numerous and varied: teaching younger children and peers, tutoring children in scholastic difficulties, helping peers cope with adolescent problems of adult alienation and drug abuse, helping runaways, aiding handicapped people of all ages, assisting in transportation, publishing newspapers bearing on matters of special community interest, and functioning as entrepreneurs and as assistants to community problem solvers.

We can cite as one example of this type of operation the "Rent-a-Kid" service of Atlanta, Georgia, where anyone wishing part-time help can call a central number and get a young person to help cut the lawn, wash the car or do other odd jobs. Another is the "Teenage Tenant Training Council" (3T's) of New York City, run by an educator from one of New York City's schools. Its legwork is implemented by fifteen-to eighteen-year-old paid workers from the Neighborhood Youth Corps, a program of the federal government. They are trained to uncover and report housing code violations, to insure that landlords are not over-charging tenants and to organize tenants' associations so that they can deal with the landlords. Clearly a responsible task requiring both knowledge and judgment, this summer program has been so successful that it has been continued under an enlarged super-visory staff of one paid adult director and two young assistants plus a secretary.

Another example is the "Youth Tutoring Youth" program originated by the National Commission on Resources for Youth, in which fourteen- and fifteen-year-olds, all of whom are below their grade in reading, get to work tutoring younger students who are also underachievers. This is done on a one-to-one basis with substantial benefit to tutor, tutees, schools and community. A critical element in the success of these programs is the positive atmosphere of people helping people.

Though we could go on at some length with these examples, we trust that we have already made the point well enough that there are many thoroughly realistic and practicable ways in which we can, if we have the will, break down and eliminate the blockades which have effectively prevented a large proportion of youth from gaining experience before they become adults, and these efforts should make the transition to that state more attrac-tive and rewarding than it has been for many in recent times.

Education also can be made more relevant to life realities by having school systems work closely with business, industry and other private enterprises. For example, at the instigation of the Boston School Board, the First National Bank of Boston and the Massachusetts General Hospital, among others, have set up programs which enable young people to participate in the adult work world in meaningful ways while still in school. Significantly, many then move into permanent jobs within these same institutions.

According to John Stetson, the programs of the First National Bank place particular emphasis on upgrading the skills of and increasing the opportunities available to high school and college students who are potential dropouts or members of minority groups who need special help in qualifying to pass the simple clerical and other skill tests administered to all job applicants. In an incentive training program for members of minority groups, the participants are hired as temporary staff members and paid a weekly salary while upgrading their skills. The rate of success for completion of training has been high, and most of the participants have then moved into full-time jobs in the bank. In the work-study programs for high school students, the day is divided between academic work at the school and work at the bank. For the hours the students work, they are paid the same salary that anyone else holding the same job would receive. Initially, most of the jobs involve either low-level clerical or messenger duties, but the bank constantly strives to upgrade and diversify the students' assignments. The bank also has a cooperative education program for college students who divide their semester periods between work and study periods. Some work in clerical capacities; others are hired as premanagement trainees. As with the high school students, these internships often lead to permanent positions within the bank. Unfortunately, *these efforts to provide young people with opportunities to upgrade themselves in the work world are all too scarce and should be universalized.*

In New York City, similar experience is being provided through a program called Executive High School Internship. In less than two years this program, administered jointly by the city's Human Resources Administration and the Board of Education, became so successful that several foundations agreed to fund a nationwide effort to set up similar projects in cities from Florida to California. The originator of the New York City program, Sharlene Pearlman Hirsch, previously had developed internship programs for people in their midthirties, but became convinced that such opportunities should be made available at a much earlier age. She persuaded Jule Sugarman, director of the Human Resources Administration, to try out the idea with high school students. Twenty commissioners and various city agencies agreed to serve as sponsors for one high school student each. The young people were selected without regard to race, scholastic standing, social or economic position, the principal criterion being that they were boys and girls who, for one reason or another, were not using their full potential in their high school work. Under the stimulus of being given real responsibility in the real world, some of these young people became so enthusiastic that they would show up for work during weekends and off-hours as well as during their scheduled time, even though they received no salaries. So well did they meet their responsibilities that some became indistinguishable from regular, permanent employees. (Indeed, when I met one of these interns on a visit to Mr. Sugarman's office, I assumed that the young man was Mr. Sugarman's principal assistant.) After spending a semester on a working sabbatical from their studies, many of the students returned to their classrooms with a new sense of purpose for the education they had previously considered an unproductive bore.

From the initial tentative commitment to the placement of twenty students in the fall of 1971, the program in New York City in 1972 involved more than seven hundred students from sixty-six different high schools. These interns worked closely with the executives and officers of hospitals, museums, department stores, advertising agencies, television studios, civic groups, business corporations, newspapers and government agencies. By the end of 1973, programs in nine other cities were well on their way. This program has done much to break down the prejudice against employment of teenagers as apprentice-partners to adults. The enthusiasm of employers for the program demonstrates that it is not a one-way handout for the benefit of young people; both the adults and the young people profit from the association and learn from each other.

A great deal can be gained also by attending educational

institutions which lie outside, but alongside, the classic formal schools. One example is provided by the North Bennett Street Industrial School of Boston, which was the first of its type in America. Founded by Pauline Agassiz Shaw in 1881, it was designed to provide young men with an opportunity to learn a trade by means other than conventional apprenticeships.

To attend, you must be sixteen years or older — the oldest on record thus far was eighty. You must be able to communicate — hear *or* read, speak *or* write; to see and to use tools. Most important, you must also be eager to learn a trade regardless of what difficulties may lie in your way. This particular school has always taught skills suited to the times. At present, they are running classes in cabinet and furniture making, camera repair, carpentry, drafting, jewelry making and repair, offset printing, sheet metal working and watch repair. Many students take a brief basic vocational course first — one designed to uncover an individual's abilities, aptitudes and interests. Classes are small: fifteen or so students working under the guidance of an expert craftsman, who quietly insists on excellence of workmanship — and gets it! The place is serene, the atmosphere happy and positive. The costs of tuition are low, about $2,000. After a year of this kind of schooling, these people are able to get well-paying jobs — up to $15,000 a year to start with — in trades which are in short supply.

One of the most exciting aspects of this situation is the fact that it should be possible to replicate institutions of this sort widely at low cost in towns and villages across the land by taking advantage of the skills represented among craftsmen in the area who have an interest in cultivating in others, male and female, young and old, the skills they have acquired over the years. It fosters communication between generations! It keeps people busy, creatively and usefully. By preparing them for jobs that are open, it fills a social need. It is not constrained by the fixed requirements that typify degree-granting institutions. On the other hand, pupils are accredited for their accomplishments by a certificate.

In all the foregoing connections, to avoid the distress which so frequently accompanies being both unemployed and poor, Mary

Rowe urges that ways be found to attach paychecks to socially constructive and personally satisfying occupations that people design for themselves. People have to have money. They have to eat. But, instead of continuing with the indignity of welfare handouts, it seems preferable to encourage people of all ages to propose projects which they believe will better the community, the lives of other people or society as a whole. These projects could range widely from such diverse activities as helping children, elderly or handicapped people who are in need of help, to turning unhappy areas into parks, to creating new and valuable services, and so forth almost ad infinitum. These proposals could be reviewed by a committee of local residents whose integrity and freedom from personal conflicts of interest are beyond question. This committee would be empowered by the local government to authorize support of approved projects in the form of skilled guidance, necessary raw materials and minimum wages for those who wish to do the work. All this would be with the proviso that the proponents do what they propose to do in a reasonably capable and efficient manner.

This could be done without introducing great numbers of people into the overloaded labor market. First of all, most of these people would be doing jobs that are now going undone. Second, much of their pay would be coming from tax funds now devoted to old-fashioned welfare allotments rather than from private enterprise. The key issue, however, is not the source of funds so much as it is making it financially possible to do things that they and other people recognize as socially constructive to all concerned.

In closing, we are drawn to the conclusion that the preschool and school programs for children and youth should be reoriented, away from the goal of readying the majority for college to one of making sure that all have learned a great deal about how to deal capably with the problems of everyday adult existence. Implicit in this thesis is the concept that they be both exposed in constructive and interesting ways to the three R's and other essential fundamentals and provided with opportunities to learn what it is like to contribute to as well as to receive from others, to perform significant jobs responsibly and to fill in one's spare time enjoyably through participating in sports and/or arts. They also need to learn about the fact that we exist on a planet of finite dimensions and limited resources which took ages to create and can easily be lost in a relatively few moments to everyone if not properly guarded and conserved.

Inherent also is the thought that the objective of preparing as many children as possible for college or for high managerial posts has been greatly overdone. As we noted earlier, the majority have no real need for, and derive little benefit — even vicariously — from college and postcollege graduate education. On the contrary, those that go through all the expense and toil of obtaining an advanced degree and wind up jobless and devoid of even the simplest kinds of marketable manual, technical or business skills are apt to be extremely frustrated, restive people. This is not just a matter of erroneous estimates of need for high-level brain power. It is also a function of the fact that our nation has tended to overemphasize personal affluence, power and prestige and underrate the joys that accrue from performing well in comfortable association with one's friends and workaday associates in one of the numerous well-paid, pragmatic roles that must be filled if life is to be an almost universally gratifying experience.

Over and above all these considerations lies the reality that young people are not likely to *want* to join the work world when they become adults unless many of the criteria drawn up by Renato Tagiuri as set forth above are approached quite closely. This means that there is no way of escaping from the reality that those responsible for the design and operation of adult work arrangements, whether they intend this to be so or not, are going to continue to exert a major influence upon the work orientation of young people from the time they first become aware of this aspect of life.

# 8

---

## Have Ethics Become Outmoded?

Ethics, as commonly defined, have to do with the principles of "right" or "good" conduct. They encompass morals which are concerned with the application of ethical principles to human conduct in everyday living. This topic would be relatively easy to deal with if one could be as absolute about ethical principles and the application of them to human decision-making as one can be, for example, of the position of the sun and the stars as points of reference for navigating a ship.

The struggle between good and evil has fascinated mankind since the dawn of history. Stories of valor and sacrifice have been part of fables and folklore and the subjects of mythology handed down from generation to generation. The triumph of good over evil has been at the root of all the great religions, and the upward and downward pull on man has forever been a subject for philosophers, novelists and poets. Although there are times when we realize that we are doing things which we ought not to be doing or are failing to do things which we should be doing, there is something inherent in mankind which gives most people an urge to behave decently despite all their temptations, faults and failures. In its highest interpretation this urge has been referred to as "divine restlessness." In its most practical sense, it can be considered to be an intrinsic drive toward social behavior which is compatible with survival.

It has been noted by Edward Wilson and others that altruistic behavior is important to the socialization and group life, not only of man, but of other species as well. Elephant "aunts" watch over pregnant females, and later when the young are born, help to care for and protect the young. Not only do the parents of wolf cubs care for them, but an uncle will bring them food and help teach them how to hunt. Even baboons will sacrifice their lives to keep a predatory leopard from attacking a sleeping group of baboons in the band to which they belong. Thus the group is protected by the individual through some basic drive which is probably inborn and essential ultimately for survival.

One can get some insight into the ways in which people have evolved ethical principles and moral guidelines over the centuries from Lawrence Kohlberg's analysis of the stages of moral development that children go through as they grow up.

At birth and during the early months of life, children's behavior is instinctively directed egocentrically to make sure that their own needs for attention, care and nourishment are satisfied. Meanwhile, they are endowed with a latent capacity to evolve along altruistic, ethical lines through a series of stages to the point where some realize that fair play, concern for the welfare of others and striving for goals that transcend selfish interests are essential to satisfaction with life and successful coexistence on this planet.

The first of the "moral stages" to become apparent after children develop some control over their behavior is characterized by orientation to punishment and reward and to physical and material power. Anything that children are told by parents and other authoritarian figures at this early stage is viewed by them as good.

The second is dominated by the doctrine that pleasure derived as a result of immediate gratification is the chief good in life. One discerns here beginning notions of reciprocity, but with emphasis on exchange of favors: "You scratch my back and I'll scratch yours." These first two stages are considered to be "preconventional" because decisions are made on the basis of self-interest and material considerations; they are typical of young children and delinquent older ones.

At the third stage, there is a shift toward seeking to meet expectations and winning approval of one's immediate group by being a "good child." As a result morality becomes defined by the relationship which one has with one's colleagues. Anything which is acceptable to them is deemed to be good. This acceptableness may be evidenced in behavior which is "good" according to the codes set up by the "establishment." In this case, the resultant behavior is likely to be viewed approvingly by society as a whole. On the other hand, when young people break away from home as a result of feeling alienated from their parents and then join up with a gang of likeminded peers, their behavior is not apt to conform to what the "establishment" considers to be good. Indeed, there is a strong tendency for nonmoral or amoral value systems to fill the psychosocial deficit which develops when parents fail to maintain a substantial, positive relationship with their children.

The fourth stage is marked by alignment toward authority, law and duty, and to maintaining a fixed order, whether social or religious. Those who advocate the supremacy of law and order regardless of circumstances operate at this level. These group-oriented stages three and four are the "conventional" ones, within which most of the adult population operates.

The fifth stage is directed towards a social contract — that is, to the protection of the rights of others by the establishment of a democratic order that favors social equality. This is exemplified by the American Constitution and its Bill of Rights. Principled, altruistic behavior based on the tenets set forth by other persons becomes noticeable for the first time at this stage.

Those who function at the sixth level have worked out a principled philosophy which includes a consistent set of beliefs. This level resembles stage five in that it involves principles of justice based on equal respect for all persons. This is, however, the only level where people respond primarily to their own consciences in making moral judgments. An example of this stage is found in those who refuse to bear arms in wartime because of conscientious objections to killing other human beings under any circumstances. These two, final, "principled" stages are found only in 10 to 20 percent of the adult population, of whom only 5 percent reach stage six.

The fact that children growing up in places as diverse as the United States, Great Britain, Mexico, Turkey, Taiwan and Malaysia follow the same pattern of moral development indicates that we are dealing with a fundamental component of human nature. At the same time, the fact that only a few reach the most advanced stages, coupled with our own observations that people tend to slide back a stage or more in their conduct when greatly stressed by illness, fatigue or the like, suggests that it requires a good deal of personal effort to attain and maintain a high level of moral conduct.

They also imply that even though there probably is some tendency for children to evolve along moral lines, the urge to do so instinctively and spontaneously is not strong enough on the average to outbalance temptations to satisfy selfish desires. It follows that if the adult members of society want their children to evolve along ethical lines, they must be prepared to exemplify high levels of moral thinking and behavior in their own daily lives, to support their children when they display readiness to do likewise and to discipline them when necessary.

This brings us to a crucial question — how do people distinguish between decisions and actions that are good rather than evil, right rather than wrong, just instead of unjust? For centuries, people have been searching for such ethical universals — that is, for expressions of ethical principles which can be used as guidelines under any and all situations. Though it never may be possible to satisfy everyone with any single set of principles, there are two which seem to have stood the test of time since they were first set forth in the ancient scriptures. Paraphrased, the first holds that human beings should strive for goals which transcend their own personal, selfish interests. And the second maxim implies that we should be as concerned for the well-being of our fellow man as we are for our own. It is interesting to note how closely the attitudes and behaviors represented in Kohlberg's stages five and, especially, six conform to these two venerable precepts.

They also are reflected to a striking degree in many of the steps taken by Americans to right wrongs by eliminating slavery, abusive child-labor practices, abject poverty, racial discrimination and inequities in opportunities for women and men to work for equal pay. All these are representative of situations in which a creative and involved minority called attention to injustice. In due course — and this may take more than a generation — these are being recognized as such and subsequently acted upon by the majority. Ethical principles have their roots in people who may be reacting in the only way that is compatible with human survival.

Be that as it may, students of moral and ethical issues like to point out the dilemmas which people may face in which there appear to be no ethically sound solutions. For instance, we can cite the classic postulation of a situation faced by a husband whose wife has developed a disease from which she will soon die unless a truly effective remedy is applied without delay. The only known cure for this disease is a newly discovered drug, of which only enough is available to cure one person. The pharmacist who owns this supply has set a very high price on it. The husband cannot afford to pay this price, and the pharmacist refuses to sell it at a discount. The question is — what is the right thing for the husband to do under these circumstances? Should he steal the drug and thereby save his wife's life, or should he adhere to ethical principles of lawful behavior and respect for the rights of others at the cost of losing his wife?

Suppose now that the husband decides on an unethical course of action to save his wife. But what if, when he sets out to steal the drug, he discovers three other men with similar problems who also have decided that thievery is not as bad as allowing one's wife to die. Does he now kill his three competitors in order to save *his* wife? And, when all has been said and *done,* what if it turns out that the pharmacist had invested all he had in this drug in an effort to make enough money to pay for the surgery that *his* wife needed to remain alive and well?

The trouble with these postulates of situational ethics is that they leave no room for working out ethically and morally reasonable alternative solutions. However, they do serve to highlight the kind of intellectualized reasoning which people sometimes use to justify doing what they want regardless of the effects upon others of their acts.

As we look around us now and contemplate the widespread

preoccupation with materialistic goals, political and monetary power, the record high rates of crime on the streets, warfare in the schools, fractionation of families and so on, it is hard to escape the conclusion that our society taken as a whole is functioning at a low ebb as far as adherence to ethical principles is concerned. We will have more to say about these matters in the final chapter. Meanwhile we would like to consider some of the moves which we might make to counter these costly and dangerous trends.

We note first that cultivation of morality in a child is a highly personal task. Since it has to do with the quality of behavior which people exhibit and with the effects which this quality has upon the condition of others, it is essential that the child sees himself as a member of some coherent group. Otherwise, he cannot understand the basis for moral thought. Though this grouping should include neighborhood friends, day care centers, school and other places, we know of no satisfactory substitute for having a decent family at the core. The fact that American families have undergone drastic changes in recent decades has not diminished the importance to children of having at least one responsible, caring parental person available as needed. This person must be there not only during the early, heavily dependent years, but also subsequently while the children are learning how to be self-sufficient.

Next in importance is the character of those to whom the child looks for guidance and modeling. Parents and others who are maladjusted themselves, who are at war with each other, who behave in amoral ways, automatically transmit these traits to their children. It serves little good for a father to order a child to be nice to his mother and then go out and get drunk and later come home to curse and yell and, perhaps, even hit her himself. Neither does it help if a parent demands that a child be honest and truthful at one moment and at another teaches him how to cheat at the turnstile or to shoplift, or to give short change. And failure to admonish and, when indicated, punish children for stealing cookies out of boxes on supermarket shelves can be almost as demoralizing as overt training in thievery. But it does contribute to a child's moral development when a mother or father serves as a dependable source of affectionate concern and teaches a child how to care for himself and others, and how to get along in mutual trust and faith.

Children also need to have the experience of knowing what it is like to possess some material things, such as toys or clothes or books or tools or money, which they value. If they have never owned anything they really cherish and can be proud of, they have no way of knowing what it is like to have something stolen or destroyed maliciously. It follows that under these circumstances they are not likely to have much respect for property belonging to others. In line with this idea is the fact that youngsters who are apprehended for acts of theft, vandalism, mugging and the like often give a history of having been brought up in a broken home, or by parents who themselves were behaving in criminal or otherwise amoral, antisocial ways, or under circumstances where they had little to be proud of and hence little to lose.

Schools also can play a very constructive role as far as the moral development of children is concerned. So too can scouting, camping, church groups, team activities, 4-H groups and the like. For example, they can provide opportunities for young people to learn the elements of altruistic cooperation through functioning as teammates. In these regards it can be very helpful to have a common cause to work for. For example, in Viet Nam, where the trees had been denuded by warfare, they have involved the very old and the very young in a massive tree-planting effort. This is giving the very young, who until socialized tend to be destructive, an opportunity to invest their energies in making things grow. For the old, likewise, even though they may not reap fruit from the trees they are planting side by side with the children, there is the satisfaction of knowing that they are building for the next generation.

Schools can also provide the young with opportunities to learn how people can compete fairly and squarely, both individually and collectively to everyone's advantage. Children can do so as members of classroom teams, sports teams, business enterprises and the like. They also can compete as writers, dancers, musicians, artists, dressmakers and so forth. We emphasize this because more than a few people have developed such a negative attitude about cutthroat forms of competition that they would like to eliminate competition altogether from the American scene. In the first place, we doubt that this could ever be accomplished, and in the second place, we are convinced that human beings need to compete in various ways to remain strong and healthy physically and mentally. But this does not mean that foul as well as fair ways and means should be tolerated.

Unfortunately, there is considerable reason to be concerned about the fairness represented in the attitudes and behavior of some school and group leaders. This was exemplified by the headmaster of a school, who was heard to say recently that he "did not want to start worrying about whether he was being fair to teachers, or whether his teachers were being fair to pupils, or whether pupils were fair to each other." It has also been reflected in the behavior of teachers who, in their classrooms, ignore or explicitly denigrate disadvantaged students and nurture a false sense of superiority among others, thereby creating an atmosphere of hostility and inequity rather than of justice and mutual concern. By contrast, there are many schools where this kind of amorality is supplanted by a requirement that pupils regularly examine issues and think out fair and equitable solutions along the lines described earlier in connection with George Richmond's microsociety school. In other words, the schools can and should be striving to make consideration of moral issues a normal habit of life which one applies continuously to oneself in judging and deciding what's the best thing to do.

In dealing with topics like ethics and moral behavior, one can sometimes gain perspective by taking a look at the opposite. In this case this would be amorality, as represented in acts which are criminally unfair, unjust, inimical, injurious and uncalled-for.

Children are not immune from amoral ways of thinking and behaving. But society has been reluctant to apply the word *criminal* to children before they have attained an age where they theoretically should know the difference between right and wrong, good and bad. So the term *delinquent* has been chosen and applied to those who, as children, have committed acts which would be labeled criminal if they had been done by adults.

Studies of large groups of children, such as the Philadelphia Youth Cohort Study, which followed about 10,000 boys, born in 1945, from the age of six to the age of eighteen, have disclosed that as many as 40 to 50 percent of our young people get into trouble with the police at least once during their preadult years. Acting on the premise that their misbehavior was intrinsically "bad," the usual method of management by the courts has been to give them a warning after the first offense, if it was not too serious, and to place them on probation, or, after the second or third offense, send them to a training school. It is interesting to note that, whether because of or in spite of these punitive measures, after two or three such encounters about 95 percent of these youngsters stop misbehaving and become reasonably well adjusted adult members of society.

In many instances, behavior such as this probably represents nothing more than the natural tendency young people have to explore and test their physical and social environment. But, one has to recognize that the nature and prevalence of amoral and antisocial behavior may be influenced by a variety of environmental factors. In saying this, we are excluding intentionally the relatively unusual instances of misbehavior which are the results of epileptic seizures, brain tumors, gross mental retardation and the like. In doing so, we are assuming that appropriate medical measures will be taken to recognize, remedy, control or protect the patient in accordance with his specific needs.

We have already mentioned above most of the potentially harmful environmental factors: that is, a highly permissive home atmosphere; a model of infidelity; cheating or unjust behavior on the part of one or both parents; parental neglect or hostility toward their children; lack of enough interesting things to do in the home, school or neighborhod; lack of ways and means to earn pocket money, to be a responsible person and to be creative personally; being a stranger in a community of strangers where no one — except the police — knows who you are or cares what you do and, last but not least, heavy exposure to sensuous sexuality, brutality, violence and temptingly expensive glamorousness on the TV screen. The remarkable thing is that so many of those who get into trouble with the law enforcement system stop misbehaving overtly after they have been apprehended two or three times. Though it is likely that some of these individuals simply become smart enough to cover up their misdeeds, we are optimistic to the point of believing that the majority have learned that society will not tolerate misbehavior beyond certain limits, and they proceed to live within those bounds.

Unfortunately, however, there remains a small but very worrisome group who continue to behave, increasingly, in criminal ways. Whereas it may be presumed that the majority of those who straighten out early in the game have a passably satisfactory home base, we know that, with few exceptions, those who keep getting into serious difficulty come from very troubled homes, where they have been grossly deprived during the early years of their childhood. A typical example would be a home where the children experienced a high degree of indifference and hostility from the parents, particularly from the father. Frequently, they are children who have observed their parents shoplifting and shortchanging and/or have themselves been taught to cheat, steal and so forth. This predisposes to attitudes toward property, particularly other people's property, which makes it very easy for them to neutralize any restraints. Today's "rip-off" psychology is an attitude toward property born of an impersonal society in which you can depersonalize the property of others to such an extent that you can appropriate it with no twinge of conscience.

This type of social environment also tends to produce a personality which has a built-in incapacity for identifying emotionally with other people in their situations; the world of people becomes a world of objects. This is particularly true with people who have been treated brutally by their parents or other mentors. The result is that they do not feel the constraints against violence toward others which ordinarily arise in people as a consequence of picturing themselves in the prospective victim's position. Children like this grow up treating their classmates with violence. For example, in school, they might beat up younger children and take their money. They cannot be controlled by authority figures, and parents bring them frequently to detention centers, complaining that they are ungovernable and incorrigible. It is tragic but true that one frequently finds that youths who have committed crimes of violence do not feel remorse for their acts. They don't feel guilty. They might even laugh about what they have done. They have very little regard for their victims, who are to them objects to play with, sadistically. It is this which above all else makes us recoil in horror.

According to Lloyd Ohlin, there are widespread gaps in the availability of services needed to keep these more difficult and dangerous juvenile delinquents out of trouble, to say nothing of habituating them to a socially acceptable life-style. For one thing, the courts and correctional institutions are overwhelmed by the number of cases they have to handle; they lack sufficient financial and physical resources. But what is perhaps more important, they are not sure what measures are really effective.

This is reminiscent of a medical condition which was widespread among children only a few decades ago, before people recognized and eliminated the *cause* of the disease. I have in mind Vitamin D–lack rickets, which characteristically results in a marked bowing of the legs and other major skeletal deformities in babies and growing children. It was learned early on that one could gain very little by attempting to correct the malformations by orthopedic surgery alone. But, once the cause was recognized and the missing vitamin was then provided by one means or another, the children tended to heal themselves. If the disease had not advanced too far, the recovery would be essentially complete. If, however, the condition had become extremely deep-seated as a result of a prolonged deprivation of the essential vitamin, it might be necessary to provide both the vitamin and corrective surgical measures. Unfortunately, under these circumstances, it was very likely that the child would continue to be at least partially deformed for life. The obvious conclusion to be drawn from this comparison is that by far the most effective and least expensive way to avoid this type of misfortune is by preventing it in the first place by making sure that children's essential needs are met. In the case of rickets, it is for Vitamin D. In delinquent youngsters, the essential need appears to be for the basic social and psychological supplies which fortunate children get from their parents, teachers and friends.

The truth of this theory is becoming more and more apparent as experts in juvenile delinquency are finding that punitive treatment of seriously delinquent youths is not likely to improve their behavior. On the contrary, all indications show that the incarceration of youth with other experienced criminals is an almost sure way to guarantee that they will become skilled and hardened criminals themselves. And imprisonment is expensive. In saying this, we are not suggesting that no penalties should be imposed upon people who steal, destroy valuable property, or the like. Indeed, we feel that the courts have, if anything, been too lenient. But we do consider it essential that criminality be changed from profitable to an unprofitable activity to the fullest extent possible by requiring juveniles and others to devote a fair fraction of their energies to repaying, in dollars earned or public services rendered, those they have victimized. For instance, burglars who have been caught redhanded after having looted a house and disposed of valuable property may be turned loose by the courts with no penalty other than being placed on probation. They manage thus to profit appreciably and almost painlessly from their criminal activities. Under such circumstances, why should they mend their ways?

The question is, how can society develop better and more universally available ways for providing people, especially children who are being socially deprived and injured in their own homes, with a decently supportive alternative? Massachusetts and a number of other states are in the process of trying to do just this in the hope of finding a better way to deal with youthful delinquents than the standard training school and prison regimens. For example, if state officers feel the family is capable of responding favorably, they may try to shore it up with homemaker guidance services to the extent that it seems reasonable for the child to continue to live at home. If they do not consider the prospects at home promising, they might try to place the youngster in a foster or small group home where the family is made up at least in part of nondelinquent youths. Living under these circumstances, a troubled youth may learn as much from his peers as from anyone else about how to develop emotional relationships and to think about the welfare of others besides himself. Delinquent youths can also be urged to set up and apply, of their own free will, guidelines for solving problems involving justice, honor, trust and so on. From these types of "encounter" experiences with mates of the same age, young people begin to perceive themselves as being aided by other people who are responsive to them, and their reaction is often, "I'm being helped and this is a good thing — these are good people — they care about me." This just marks the beginning of their healing, however, because they can fall back rapidly to old ways of thinking and behaving if they are turned loose before they have had a chance to become well-established as valued members of a well-respected family of people.

This process may take periods of months to years, depending upon each situation, but we believe that even at current going rates of $2,000 to $3,000 per child per year, treatment based on this kind of exposure to a good family-home environment is relatively inexpensive and most importantly it is much more likely to prove beneficial than old-fashioned, primarily punitive methods. We believe that it is going to be of the utmost importance to bear in mind that, as with rickets, the possibilities for a satisfactory outcome are enormously better when a pathogenic situation is recognized and corrected early than when problems are allowed to become deeply entrenched. And, even though this thesis is now being given a thorough test in Massachusetts and a few other states, it is going to take several years to determine how effective the new approach is going to be.

In previous pages of this volume, we talked about the fact that many of the children who are growing up today in modern America lack substantial opportunities to become engaged in service which gives them a sense of being useful, of having contributed to others in ways which are obviously valuable, of having helped to create or maintain something in which they can have a sense of personal pride in accomplishment. The same is true as regards opportunities for young people to earn pocket money in honorable ways.

In view of this lack, we believe that serious consideration should be given to the possibility of requiring all children, boys and girls, young men and women alike, to devote a certain amount of time, or, perhaps alternatively, earn a certain number of credit points, by serving the needs of the community in which they are living. To avoid the dangers inherent in a politically managed youth service system — such as that engineered by Hitler — it would appear wise to have this implemented as an integral part of the school curriculum, with the primary aim of engendering a sense of responsibility to society through rendering some necessary community service.

Even though it may be necessary to centralize overall responsibility for the maintenance of standards, the program should be managed by respected local citizens who might be invited to serve as members of local boards in much the same manner that men and women served on Selective Service Boards during World War II. The risk of multiplying our already gigantic bureaucracy could be minimized by mediating a great deal of the planning and implementation of such a program through the schools along the lines outlined in Chapter 7.

The boards, working in collaboration with the school system and with professional assistance, would be responsible for developing a series of tasks which young people should be able to perform with some, but not much, supervision. For example, they could be set to work cleaning up the streets and byways of metropolitan areas which are unkempt, preparing and delivering meals for homebound and elderly people, assisting in the care of younger children in day care centers, parks and playgrounds, serving as student aides in museums and libraries, repainting public vehicles and so forth. If children are living in an area where no such opportunities are possible or conceivable, it should be arranged for them to serve alternately in some other needy community. Becoming aware of the possibilities, young people could come up with ideas and projects on their own that could be of value to the community.

Senior citizens of good repute who have the time, sound health and appropriate temperamental makeup could derive satisfaction through functioning as supervisors of these activities to the benefit of all concerned, both materially and socially. While the bulk of the expenses would necessarily have to be borne by us as taxpayers, no obstacles should be placed in the way of developing equitable working arrangements with nonprofit, private agencies. Under these circumstances, the agency would be expected to reimburse the state for the services rendered. The state in turn should recompense the children and their supervisors in some appropriate manner, thereby providing both with some of the pocket money which they need so urgently.

Obviously, it would be unwise to attempt to implement such a program on a nationwide basis without first having tried it out tentatively on a small scale in a variety of communities. At the same time, we would like to emphasize that we would not have felt inclined to submit ideas along these lines were it not for the fact that we are paying an extremely high price for our present drift away from ethical considerations.

This, of course, has always been one of the great problems of the human condition. But it has become increasingly critical because of the fact that people now have so much more capacity to destroy and to injure, not only those who live in the immediate neighborhood, but almost everybody on earth. It was interesting to read in *The New York Times* a short while ago about how the President of the United States always has within easy reach a small black box which contains the apparatus for signaling the release of atomic weaponry. No doubt other heads of state have similar black boxes. That a few people today have the capacity to destroy almost everything that anybody cares about, within the space of an hour or two, makes clear the modern reality that our whole civilization hangs on the *decisions* of people as to whether they're going to *behave* according to ethical or unethical principles. So, even though these are among the most intangible of all the issues we have been discussing in this volume, they float to the top as among the most, if not the most, crucial. Interestingly, they keep cropping up in a variety of forms as we move along from considering the issues which surround raising children while they are young to those which obtain when they are older. There is really very little difference between the topics we have been discussing in this chapter and those we were considering a few chapters back in connection with the inculcation early in infancy of an outgoing, caring concern for others.

# 9

## Keeping Children Alive and Well

As Benjamin Disraeli remarked in a speech delivered on July 24, 1877, "The health of the people is really the foundation upon which all the happiness and all their powers as a state depend." Though the nature and causes of disease have changed greatly, the concept that health is one of the most fundamental of all human attributes is as valid today as it was a hundred years ago.

In approaching this subject, it is helpful to remember that the great majority of children are endowed at conception with the potential for developing along sound lines into healthful adults. Attainment of this potential is, however, contingent upon being protected against major injuries and being appropriately nourished, housed, clothed and otherwise cared for physically, psychologically and socially. It follows that if we as parents and health care professionals hope to raise generations of healthy, competent adults we must be concerned as much with cultivating wellness as with curing diseases and repairing injuries.

This is not a novel thought. As early as 1874, at the founding meeting of the American Public Health Association, A. P. Barnard, president of Columbia College, was moved to remark:

Such has been the success of modern measures for closing up all the insidious approaches by which disease had hitherto affected its entrance into the family, the community or the individual organism as to encourage a hope even so seemingly wild and visionary that the time is coming in which disease itself shall be utterly extinguished and men shall begin to live out the days which heaven intended for them.

When that time arrives, if it ever shall, your honorable and learned profession may find, like Othello, its occupation gone, but it will be itself which will have destroyed it and which will have established, in doing so, a nobler title to the gratitude of mankind than all its untiring labors for the relief of suffering humanity through centuries of self-sacrificing devotion hitherto have already run.

This still is our aim. But it is now clear that it is far beyond the capabilities of any profession to accomplish this by itself. For one thing, health is a function of the physical, chemical and biological phenomena with which American medicine has been concerning itself almost exclusively in recent years. For another it is dependent upon a variety of behavioral, psychological, social, economic, technological and political factors.

We can illustrate this idea by recounting the history of a young girl aged seven who was brought to us with the complaint of marked dwarfism. No intrinsic physical, metabolic or endocrine abnormality could be found to explain her condition, but it was noted that she was quite thin and underweight for her height. At the actual age of seven years, she corresponded in height to normal girls of four years and in weight to normal girls of two years. This finding led to explorations of the possibility that her dwarfism might be overcome if she would eat enough. It was possible to demonstrate under carefully controlled conditions that this was true. Thus it appeared that undernutrition was the immediate cause of her dwarfism. This was not the whole story, however, for it became clear that though there were ample supplies of food at home, she had a very poor appetite. The cause of this lack of appetite in turn was found to be social in nature. She was living in a foster home, having been placed there after removal from her own neglectful parents by the state's Division of Child Guardianship. The foster mother was very fond of the child, who reciprocated her affection. Because of this affection and the fact that there was an ever-present threat that they might be separated by the state authorities, the foster mother had undertaken to adopt the girl. However, the foster mother was blocked in her adoption efforts by rulings to the effect that because this child was physically abnormal she was not a suitable candidate for adoption.

This ruling served to sustain a vicious cycle of insecurity, separation anxiety, loss of appetite, poor caloric intake, dwarfism, insecurity, and so on. Demonstration to the authorities of the self-perpetuating nature of these relationships led to approval of the adoption. This approval in turn was followed by marked spontaneous gains in weight and height, gains that were unobtainable by use of drugs, hormones or direct dietary recommendations. This child is representative of many others in whom stunting of physical, intellectual and psychological development can be traced to a web of interlocking biophysical and sociobehavioral factors.

The essential nature of social and psychological supplies as companions to dietary and other vitally important physical supports has also been demonstrated on groups of children. One of the most convincing studies was that reported in 1973 and 1974 by Harrison McKay and associates on groups of preschool children living in the lowest socioeconomic areas of Cali, Colombia. The purpose was to assess the effects upon their physical growth, health and psychological development of providing them only with health care plus nutritional supplementation, on the one hand, and additionally with psychological stimulation, on the other.

At the beginning of the study, these youngsters were grossly underweight and underheight in comparison with children of identical ages living at the same time in middle to upper socioeconomic sections of Cali. The deprived children were also markedly backward in relation to their more fortunate neighbors with respect to such indices of mental functioning as verbal reasoning and traditional knowledge. Providing them with health care and dietary supplements had a striking beneficial effect on their bodily appearance and general level of physical activity. Formerly skinny and listless, they became active and well-nourished even to the point of plumpness. But the study showed that providing them with nutritional and health supports alone did not help their psychological and cognitive development. This happened only after the children were provided with additional psychological stimulation in the form of personal attention, educational experiences and the like. When these were given to them, the children made major gains in the intellectual and social spheres, proving again that psychological and social supplies are as essential to the development and functioning of children's minds as material supplies are to the development and functioning of their bodies, including, of course, their brains.

We shall now pursue this concept under a series of interrelated headings.

*The influence of circumstances surrounding pregnancy on the newborn.* Even though poverty does not have directly deleterious effects on developing babies, it predisposes to the occurrence of factors which do. This is evident in the relationship between family income and infant mortality rates. The current infant mortality rate for families with annual incomes under $3,000 is 50 percent higher than our national average of nineteen per thousand live births. Even more striking are the discrepancies which have been observed between adjacent communities of different socioeconomic status. For example, it was discovered recently that the infant mortality rate in the slums of Harlem was twice the national average and three times higher than that of a nearby, affluent New York City community. Rates also vary from state to state by as much as 100 percent, depending on the state's fiscal status, the availability of medical services there, and so on. The places with the highest rates of infant mortality are those where mothers do not receive prenatal medical care. More than a million babies are born each year in this country to mothers who have not received any medical care, and most of these mothers are members of economically and socially disadvantaged families who either lack access to services, or who do not understand their importance.

Mothers who are very young in age have more complications in pregnancy than do mothers of young adult age. The chances of giving birth to an infant who is low in weight (that is, premature) are about 18 per hundred among mothers who are less than fifteen years of age, 11 per hundred for those who are fifteen to nineteen years of age and only 7 or 8 out of a hundred for mothers twenty to thirty years old. This fact is significant, because mental retardation occurs 75 percent more often among low-birth-weight babies than among full-term, normal infants. It also turns out that approximately 80 out of every hundred mentally defective children are born of impoverished parents. There are approximately three million such children living in the United States today.

It is gradually becoming possible to anticipate or diagnose disabling congenital malformations before conception or early enough in pregnancy to take advantage of the legal option to have an abortion. Down's syndrome — previously called mongolism — is one of the best known examples of a condition where prenatal diagnostic and counseling services may be of practical value. Such services are now widely available at low cost in most of the nation's major medical centers.

*The role of parents in the prevention and control of infectious disease.* One might suppose that the advantages inherent in being immunized against potentially lethal and disabling infections is so obvious that everyone would see to it that they and their children are fully immunized. However, the facts speak differently. According to the United States Center for Disease Control, nearly six million preschool children — more than a third of the fourteen million children in this age group — lack full immunization against polio, measles, rubella (German measles), diphtheria, pertussis (whooping cough) and tetanus (lockjaw). And between nine and ten million preschoolers are not protected against mumps.

This record has worsened during the past decade. For example, in 1963 84 percent of all preschool children were immunized against polio. By 1973, only 60 percent were protected. The decline is most marked among nonwhite children living in the central cities of major metropolitan areas. In the suburbs, two-thirds of the children are immunized, but in the inner city only about 40 percent are protected. Already some states are reporting increases in diseases which were thought to be well under control.

This apparent negligence is not altogether surprising, since we lack a mechanism for making certain that all children are properly immunized and for keeping accurate, up-to-date records of immunization. Physicians lack the authority to force anyone to accept preventive and therapeutic measures without explicit authorization from the courts, and this authorization is granted usually only in life-or-death situations. Since there are no public health requirements until children are in school, it is left to the parents to take care of this aspect of child health.

The fact that parents are not following through 100 percent on this matter is also not surprising. Health is so intangible. The goals and rewards of health care are so much less visible and less immediate than the many other things that are constantly competing for parents' attention, effort and money. So people coast along without doing anything unless and until illness strikes as a sharp and sometimes disastrous reminder.

Another reason why parents may fail to provide their children with protective health care is that services are often not available where they are needed or at a price which parents can afford. When such services do exist, people usually use them, sometimes with beneficial results beyond those they are actively seeking. Take, for example, the matter of acute upper respiratory tract infections. Because symptoms of acute sore throat and high fever are evident and worrisome, parents usually seek medical aid if they occur. Sometimes such symptoms are due to infection by a streptococcus germ, which can be identified through a throat culture and can be cured by treatment with penicillin. Parents are grateful for this prompt relief and therefore are conditioned to seek out and take advantage of this type of medical care. What many of them do not realize is that early diagnosis and treatment of this particular type of acute sore throat can prevent such serious long-term complications as rheumatic fever, rheumatic heart disease, nephritis and a disease of the nervous system called chorea. At this time, strep infections are still causing nearly a hundred thousand new cases of rheumatic fever yearly and approximately sixteen thousand are dying annually as a result of rheumatic heart disease.

In one study, Johns Hopkins investigators found that the incidence of rheumatic fever fell 60 percent in areas of Baltimore where comprehensive health care facilities had been available and when the incidence remained unchanged in the rest of the city. In our opinion, this is proof of the gains to be had by making health services readily available to everyone, and if doing so cannot be accomplished otherwise, we would strongly support the establishment of a National Health Service.

*Avoiding malnutrition.* Parents play a major role in protecting children against undernutrition, on the one hand, and overnutrition and obesity, on the other. Dietary insufficiencies may take the form of grossly inadequate total food intake with resultant extreme thinness, stunting of growth, apathy and generally low energy output. This syndrome is found most often among poverty-stricken families, but it is not restricted to any one socioeconomic group. Thus, the manner in which poor families deploy their financial resources between food and other things, coupled with the way in which they prepare and eat their meals, can so compensate for limitations due to poverty that their children do get enough essential nutrients to remain well-nourished. On the other hand, even when food is readily available, if well-to-do parents neglect their children, the children can become grossly malnourished.

Though undernutrition is not caused directly by poverty, it frequently is related to it. Recognizing this, the United States Department of Agriculture has taken steps to eliminate food shortages among financially disadvantaged families by means of a food stamp program. Today fifteen million people in our country receive food stamps every month through this program, which was started on a trial basis about ten years ago. Coverage used to be conditional on state participation, but it became mandatory nationwide on July 1, 1974. This mandate also required that outreach efforts be made to identify needy families who are unaware of this opportunity and make aid available to them. Though exact information concerning the effects of this program on child health is not available as yet, in view of the fact that a majority of the recipients are members of families on public assistance, it appears likely that it will go a long way toward overcoming food hunger. Unfortunately, however, it has been observed that many parents use food stamps to buy what is most expensive, but not necessarily most nutritious, like "convenience foods." In order to achieve full effectiveness, therefore, it might be necessary to develop simultaneous educational programs to help parents and others understand the importance of providing children with meals which are well-balanced and suitably prepared.

Dietary insufficiency can also take the form of one or more specific lacks under conditions where the diet is otherwise adequate or even excessive. One obvious example is dental caries, which can occur as a result of dietary fluoride insufficiency in otherwise well-nourished children. For reasons which are hard to comprehend, there are still diehard communities which remain adamantly opposed to taking the simple steps necessary to eliminate in large part the occurrence of dental caries among children — that is, by adding traces of fluoride to municipal water supplies. Somewhat less obvious is the widespread occurrence of anemia due to lack of dietary iron. Other varieties of specific dietary lack are apt to be so subtle clinically that they can be recognized only by specific laboratory tests.

All these deficiencies are in part by-products of our society's trend toward commercial production of "convenience foods," which are so highly refined that one or more necessary constituents have been lost along the way. Some of these products are so deficient in anything but calories and taste as to be little more than "junk foods." The risk here is that children will become so accustomed to eating this type of product that even if they do not develop deficiency diseases during childhood, they will have developed eating habits which may result in deficiency states in later years. The notion that one can protect against such eventualities by supplementing the diet with a pill concentrate containing all missing materials also is risky. They, too, can be deficient in essential materials, partly because we cannot be sure that our present listing of the essentials normally provided by a well-balanced diet of natural foods is complete. Conversely, plying children who are already receiving a good diet with vitamin supplements can result in overloading the body with quantities of material which they don't need, some of which become toxic when given in excess of requirements.

Obesity is another nutritional disorder which is very common in the United States. Basically, obesity is nothing more or less than excessive fatness. Many people choose to draw the line between normal and excessive weight by statistical means, such as saying that all who are more than 20 per cent overweight for their height are obese. While this is convenient, we prefer to reserve the diagnosis of obesity for those who are not only overweight, but who are also so clumsy that they are unable to participate effectively in ordinary physical activities or so unattractive that they are teased heavily and otherwise disparaged by their peers. This attitude toward obesity is so strong in the United States that one can predict that any grossly overweight children will be ranked close to the bottom in popularity by their peers. Unfortunately, this ranking compounds these children's problem by making them feel unwanted and lonely, and the temptation to compensate by eating more is great.

There are indications today that familial factors may play a role in causing obesity among children. Children who are born to parents of normal weight have a 7 percent chance of being overweight when they graduate from high school. This increases to 40 percent if one of the parents is obese and to 80 percent if both exhibit this abnormality. Some people interpret these data to signify that genetic factors play a large role in causing obesity, and they cite as supportive evidence that these parent-child weight relationships hold only for natural children, not for adopted children. Others believe equally strongly that the eating habits and physical activity modeled by parents play an equal or even more important role in causing obesity in children.

This idea is reinforced by the observation that even if one has a familial predisposition to obesity, one has, in order to become fat, to overeat relative to needs. Except among babies born to mothers who are diabetics or are incipient diabetics, it is unusual for an infant to be obese at birth. Whether they become obese subsequently is determined by the amount that they eat relative to the amounts they need to support healthy functioning, growth and development. In underdeveloped areas of the world, where food is scarce and life is hard, it is exceptional to find more than a few powerful or privileged persons who are too fat. But this problem is common in highly industrialized countries like Great Britain and the United States, where more food than is needed is readily available to the majority of the population. When this surplus is coupled with a life-style in which most of the ordinary tasks of existence are done automatically by machinery rather than by hand, where children ride rather than walk to school and sit watching TV rather than playing active games, there is a great danger of a large percentage of the population becoming over-weight. Also, unfortunately, there still is a tendency for people to assume that a good appetite and plump body signify good care and good health.

This is not true, however; obesity is a physically and socially disabling disease, which, when once established, is extremely difficult to eradicate by drugs or by psychiatric, medical or surgical means. About the only things that work are powerfully motivated self-control efforts aimed at curtailing food intake while increasing expenditures of physical energies. Occasionally one sees an adolescent become thus motivated as a result of a strong desire to be attractive to members of the opposite sex or to attain something else, such as a desirable job or position in school. One also occasionally sees obese patients lose weight to the point of emaciation when they become sick or starved for some unavoidable reasons. But these are exceptional cases. Obesity is a disease to be avoided like the plague from birth onward and especially during the early years, when eating habits, value systems and body metabolic processes are being established. Parental attitudes and behavior regarding this are of vital importance to their children's overall health.

*Accidents are expensive.* Once a child has survived the hazards of birth and the initial twelve months of life, when inborn errors are most likely to be fatal, accidents become the leading cause of death among children and account for approximately half of all the fatalities that take place between the second and nineteenth years of life. The prominence of the position held by accidents is not due to an increase in the rate at which they are happening. Actually, rates of occurrence per hundred thousand declined from seventy to thirty among one-to four-year-olds and from forty to twenty among five- to fourteen-year-old children between 1900 and 1964; however, the 1973 Statistical Bulletins of the Metropolitan Life Insurance Company and the 1975 *Accident Facts* of the National Safety Council indicate that some of this gain has been lost since 1960. This is due in part to a 26 percent upward change in deaths due to motor vehicle accidents, which head the list of specific causes of childhood injuries. Next in line are drownings and fires.

In 1973, accidents were responsible for a total of 12,500 deaths among children one to fourteen years old. During the same period, according to the National Health Survey, there were approximately twenty-five million injuries among children sixteen and under. This indicates that for every fatal accident, two thousand or more nonfatal injuries are taking place, which in turn result in about seventy-five million days of restricted activity, twenty million days of bed disability and fifteen million days lost from school. The last figure becomes more impressive when one reflects on the fact that at 180 schooldays per year, this represents a loss of eighty-three thousand child school years annually from injuries alone in the United States. At an average budgetary allotment of $2,000 per enrollee, this corresponds to the equivalent nationally of a school budget of $166 million.

Even though about 43 percent of all accidents occur in the children's own homes, it would be unfair to imply that parents could prevent all these even if they spent all day doing nothing but attending to their children, but it probably is fair to say that many of the hazards that children face are located within their homes and on the streets and play areas surrounding them. We know that many of these areas are unsafe because of fire hazards, unprotected stoves, broken glass and metal trash, improperly stored poisons, scalding water and grease within easy reach of small hands, guns left in accessible places, dangerous toys, clothing that has not been fireproofed, unregulated street crossings and so forth. While parents can reduce many of these hazards, in the final analysis control of them may require the establishment of a nationwide monitoring agency responsible for identifying conditions that threaten the safety of children and for requiring that these conditions be corrected.

*Avoiding an unnecessary sick role.* Parental attitudes can be important factors in determining the extent to which a child lives a "well" role in life as contrasted to a "sick" role. For example, we once took care of a child who developed asthma at an early age. Though this was of mild intensity, his mother thought of him as needing to be protected from the ordinary rigors of school and play life, with the result that this boy was kept out of school for some sixty-five of one hundred and sixty-five school days a year and taken to see the doctor twenty-two times in a year. Consequently, he was being disabled as severely as if he had had a major limitation in physical competence.

Children can likewise use even minor physical disabilities as a reason for not participating in activities which they find socially or physically stressful. This behavior is well exemplified by the many obese children (or their parents) who have sought — and often obtained — from pediatricians official excuses from school athletic programs.

The limitation of physical activity, such as bed rest, restriction to a wheelchair or house, can also play a significant part in a sick-role existence. In the past, many physicians and parents considered bed rest important to the treatment of respiratory infections, rheumatic fever, rheumatoid arthritis and a wide variety of other childhood illnesses. But, over the years, students have challenged these concepts, and some have found that these forms of sick role may be unnecessary and psychologically detrimental as well as less beneficial in overcoming a physical illness. It has also been found, through the close observation of children who have been hospitalized for a variety of chronic physical diseases, that they were no less active during days of "bed rest" than when allowed full activity around the ward. Children can be as lively in bed as out. Under most circumstances, however, they will limit their activities to conform to their condition, even to the point of getting into bed spontaneously when they feel ill enough.

Though it may be difficult at first, there is much to be gained if parents, with the backing of their physicians, can gradually delegate to their children more or even all of the responsibility for monitoring and treating chronic maladies like diabetes mellitus and asthma. In doing this, they will reduce the likelihood of overdoing attention and protection. They will also reduce the chances that their child will become resentful of them and antipathetic to therapy. Equally important, they will be enhancing the child's self-sufficiency and the feeling of well-being that goes with that.

*Concerning the availability and quality of health care services.* One might assume that services of such importance would be readily available to everyone in America, so that diseases could be identified and corrected before they become difficult to cure even at high expense. But this is not the way things have worked out. One reason is that our society has clung to the notion that a private health care system which relies on patient initiative can do the job. However, as we have already pointed out, physicians and other health care professionals are licensed to apply their skills only within certain closely prescribed boundaries. Health professionals must therefore rely on educational campaigns to convince people of the value of protective measures. Many such efforts are being made by the medical and nursing professions in association with educators, the media, government agencies and private foundations, businesses, industries and labor unions. And this situation would be fine if we could achieve our health goals through the gentle arts of informing and motivating parents and others responsible for the welfare of children, but it is abundantly clear that reliance on a purely voluntary system is not working in the United States today.

As things now stand, some communities are oversupplied, while others have no services at all. There are economic as well as motivational explanations for this situation. Not only for children, but for Americans of all ages, the astronomical cost of medical care is one of the principal reasons why people so often go without the services they need. For example, the average cost of a single day's hospital care now approximates $150, and in some areas is considerably higher. It is entirely possible for a middle-income family to be wiped out financially within a few days if some member has to have emergency care requiring the use of sophisticated lifesaving devices. Moreover, the long-term costs of care for a child who is chronically ill or mentally retarded are far beyond what any but the wealthiest families can absorb without severe hardship. Private medicine, like private business, cannot afford to create and maintain facilities or carry a substantial load of patients on a charity basis in a financially impoverished area. That these shortcomings are having a major impact on Americans is reflected in the fact that five-sixths of the nation's six million retarded people have never been reached by any kind of services designed to meet their special needs.

In 1972, expenditures for personal care in the United States totaled $72 billion. About a third of this came from public funds. The other two thirds came from private funds: that is, money paid by individuals to physicians, hospitals and other health caretakers and facilities, either directly or through insurance companies.

Because of the complexity and duration of the illnesses involved, by far the highest proportion of these expenditures went for the care of adults and the elderly. People sixty-five or older, who make up 10 percent of the population, accounted for 27 percent of the total spent for personal health care. People from nineteen to sixty-four years of age, who make up 52 percent of the population, accounted for 56 percent of the expenditures. *On the other hand, only 16 percent of the total expenditures went for the care of children under nineteen, who comprise 38 percent of our total population.* Only a little over a quarter of the expenditures for children and for adults come from public funds, while two-thirds of the expenditures for the elderly come from public funds.

Thus, the adults and the elderly not only consumed more health-care dollars than children, but in addition received more help from the government in meeting costs. It is fortunate that our society does recognize its obligation to share the costs of health care for needy people, who cannot possibly pay for this expense out of their limited incomes. It is also fortunate that most children, being young and sturdy, require less medical attention than older people. But what we need to think about is the sheer wastefulness of allowing major health problems to go undetected or untreated during childhood. If we chose to devote more of our health dollars — both public and private — to preventive services for children, we might forestall many of the serious, expensive physical and mental problems that make life difficult for people in their later years.

One reason why people neglect preventive care is that most private insurance plans do not cover outpatient services except when they are directly related to an illness requiring hospitalization. The recommended periodic checkup often costs at least fifty dollars and may run as high as two hundred dollars, hardly any of which is paid by insurance. Nor are people adequately covered for hospital care. Their coverage runs out at the very time when family finances are already in crisis because of loss of income of the breadwinner or the overwhelming expenses of a serious childhood disease requiring prolonged hospitalization.

The obvious solution to these problems of health care delivery is universal national health insurance. This insurance should include catastrophic-illness provisions, which would protect all families from having to bear medical costs in excess of a stated amount during any given year. It also should insure that all families be covered at reasonable cost for any type of medical care they need. The present tendency on the part of Blue Shield agencies is to refuse to pay for services rendered to patients who are well enough to be seen on an ambulatory basis. Indeed, one of the greatest faults of our present health insurance and health care delivery arrangements is that they are designed more to *treat disease* once it has occurred than to avoid disease by *cultivating and maintaining health.* In other words, we need a national *health* insurance program which would make it more profitable for health care professionals to keep people healthy than it is to treat them for diseases and disabilities after they have arisen or become well established. Among other things, such a program should permit health care professionals to treat problems in their early phases, before hospitalization is necessary. In such a program, community-based teams of physicians, nurses, social workers, psychologists or psychiatrists, dentists and others would systematically screen children and their families for health problems. These observations would then form the basis for preventive and curative measures. Furthermore, this program should be designed so that people are not denied access to national health care services as a result of upward mobility in the socioeconomic scale. On the contrary, all citizens must expect to share the costs of these services through income taxes or some other equitable channels.

*Concluding thoughts.* As one looks back over the past half-century, one can see that the causes and nature of disease among young people have been changing. At the beginning of this period, the chief causes of untimely death and disabling handicaps were infectious, nutritional, metabolic and surgical in nature. As new and better means for diagnosing, treating and preventing these primarily organic maladies have evolved, most have diminished to the point where the incidence is approaching zero. Underlying most of these gains has been the concept set forth by Abraham Flexner in 1919: that the teaching and practice of medicine should be founded firmly on the full strength of the natural sciences.

Largely as the result of the successful application of this concept we are finding now that we have a whole new set of health problems to deal with. Instead of being due primarily to unpreventable and uncontrollable organic disorders, many, indeed probably most, of the health problems posed by American children today are due to a combination of social, behavioral and organic causes. Thus, prematurity is frequently a by-product of excessive youthfulness of the mother or inadequate obstetrical care or malnutrition resulting from poverty or ignorance, or of all of these factors acting together. Mental retardation likewise occurs most often in those who have suffered these and other disadvantages as a result of being born to exceedingly youthful, impoverished and undereducated parents.

From the time when they become mobile, the leading causes of death and disability among infants and children are socio-behavioral in nature. Together, accidents, homicide, suicide, neglect and abuse account for more than two-thirds of all deaths and a large proportion of the disabilities of body and mind among children growing up in our country today. And there are many other situations where social and behavioral factors have combined with biological and physical causes to produce disease and disability among children. However, the totality of this picture is apt to be missed if health care professionals and others who work with children are not trained and alerted to recognize all the major components of these biosocial webs of causation.

The young dwarfed girl whom we described at the beginning of this chapter serves as one example of this phenomenon. She was one of the first patients who made us at the Massachusetts General Hospital aware of this kind of interplay between biological and sociobehavioral factors on an individual level. Subsequently, we conducted studies to find out how often we, as professionals trained almost exclusively in the natural sciences, were failing to look for and deal actively also with the social and environmental components of children's diseases. We concentrated on a systematically selected random sample of youngsters with chronic diseases. In each instance, the first thing we did was to search the records for the diagnoses which had been made by our usual, standard medical work-up procedures. These were then tabulated under three main headings — physical, cognitive and sociobehavioral. Then we reexamined the patients (at no cost to themselves) according to a comprehensive format designed to uncover problems in all three areas if any existed, irrespective of their primary complaint.

The results spoke for themselves. Prior to the comprehensive diagnostic survey, 96 percent of the children were considered to have one or more physical problems, while cognitive problems were recognized in 25 percent and sociobehavioral in 32 percent. After the comprehensive survey, 93 percent were still considered to have physical difficulties and 32 percent to have cognitive problems. In sharp contrast to the above, however, the proportion having sociobehavioral problems had jumped from 32 to 78 percent. In other words, when we *looked,* we found that the vast majority of these patients were suffering from combinations of physical-social-behavioral and cognitive disorders.

The physical problems included such common conditions as chronic kidney disease, recurrent pneumonia, abdominal pain, brain damage, obesity and polio. The social and behavioral problems were also familiar disorders such as antisocial behavior in the form of fire-setting and unnecessary sick roles in the form of avoidable absences from school, and they had resulted from common environmental factors such as lack of maternal care, parents fighting, fathers being depressed, et cetera.

It was not surprising that we should have missed most of the latter categories the first time around considering that in 1965–1966, when this work was done, about 95 percent of all the research and teaching resources of most major United States medical schools, including our own, were being applied to the physical and other natural science aspects of human health and disease. What is really striking is that Dr. Francis Weld Peabody was trying more than a century ago to teach young doctors to treat the "whole patient." The important factor to note is that in spite of the efforts of Dr. Peabody, Dr. Richard Cabot and others, this is still largely true today. Though there are some encouraging signs that a few changes designed to bring curricula more into line with the realities of today's patient care problems are being made, the indications are that no real push in this direction is in the immediate offing. We believe this is unfortunate, because it seems to us highly probable that success in overcoming the bulk of the health problems which are killing and hurting children in our country today is going to depend very much upon upgrading skills and resources related to the social and behavioral sciences just as acquiring a firm base in the natural sciences was fundamental to the medical education, research and practices of yesteryear. Perhaps the government's current powerful push in the direction of developing more competent generalist physicians will expedite these evolutionary adjustments.

# 10

## Perspectives and Recommendations
## for Action

W E Americans like to think of ourselves as child-loving people. But, as Marian Edelman has found in her role as director of the Children's Defense Fund, "This is a myth. Idolizing youth is not the same as placing societal priority on insuring that all children get enough food, clothing, health care, education and other services that will enable them to develop and function fully in American society. As a nation, we have failed to provide every child a chance for a decent life. We have found many children living in poverty, ignorance, ill-health and oppression. We also have found that child neglect is not limited to poor and non-white families. On the contrary, it is occurring among all ethnic and income groups."

The ways in which children can suffer serious pain, injury, disease, disability and even untimely death as a result of being disadvantaged are almost infinitely diverse. Yet they are also almost universally interrelated, representing as they do aberrations in the attitudes and behavior of the people who make up their social environment. It is fortunate that most have to do with one or more of the half dozen sets of essential material and psychosocial supplies outlined at the beginning of this volume, for it means that the origins of the problems encountered are at least approximately identifiable. This is an essential first step in developing dependable measures for preventing and curing disorders.

It follows that we must be prepared at the practical level to deal with the entire span of the child-raising and -rearing process. As noted before, this process reaches back even to the childhood of those who subsequently become parents. This is the time when people must become aware of the implications inherent in undertaking to bear and raise children. In these days when sensuous sexuality is being flaunted everywhere — in advertisements, on TV and in movies, books and clothes, it also has become imperative that children, as well as adults, know how to postpone conceiving their children until they are completely ready to become parents. Yet our society is still behaving like an ostrich with its head in the sand by prohibiting family planning agencies and physicians from dispensing birth control information and resources to children unless they already have become pregnant or have developed venereal disease. The result is that those who can least afford or are least able to carry the burdens of pregnancy, abortion or parenthood are the most likely to suffer from them because of socially imposed ignorance about reproduction. We do not wish to suggest that we support the dispensation of birth control information and methods because we are in favor of free love among our youth. Rather, we are saying that it is unrealistic to continue to treat sexually mature children as if they were immune to the seductive material which is flooding the eyes and ears of the American public.

Once s/he is born, every child needs to have a sense of belonging to at least one parental person and preferably also to a "family" of some sort. Unfortunately, for the reasons outlined earlier, many are lacking this fundamental social support. Many of these reasons are understandable, and to some extent valid, given the life problems of working parents. On the other hand, many appear to be avoidable. For instance, instead of having twenty-five of the approximately twenty-six million children who are receiving day care placed in unlicensed — that is, uncertified — centers, agencies and so forth, it should be possible to screen all child care facilities that are open to the general public, and to insist that they conform to certain minimum standards. And these standards could and should be concerned as much with the child's development as a social being as with his safety as a physical being.

When it comes to guidance, education and the setting and modeling of value systems, one finds that the task of preparing children to live successfully in today's world has become highly diversified and dispersed. At the core are the communicative and mathematical skills which people need to transmit and receive information and to think and to solve problems rationally. Also basic is knowledge of the physical world and of the workings and requirements of the human body. The same is true with regard to the social world, human psychology and social relations, ethical principles and governance. Then there is the matter of cultivating marketable skills through making arrangements for students to learn a trade by working as apprentices or to lay the foundations for a profession while still studying in the framework of the school system.

School should also be a place where young people learn how to work as members of teams and to compete honorably with others. This type of learning should include experience in judging and dealing equitably with transgressors of rules, regulations and ethical standards of conduct. Schools can also contribute greatly to the lives of young people by providing them with "eye-opener" experiences in the fields of sports, artistry, nature, fishery, town planning, architecture, government, politics, business, economics, dressmaking, cooking and so forth. Skills gained in any of these areas can enrich greatly the lives of the many who later on find it necessary to earn their living through jobs which in themselves are neither particularly interesting nor personally fulfilling.

This type of broad-based education is now being provided in those relatively few communities where school boards, teachers and parents are aware of the children's overall needs and have the determination and resources required to meet them. However, this is far from the case in thousands of other communities, where those in control are either unaware of what is at stake, or are unconvinced that this kind of investment is worthwhile. Still other communities would love to take advantage of new concepts but lack the necessary resources.

There is also the necessity of having jobs ready and waiting for young people to fill. It has been well said that nothing is so disheartening as finding that one is not needed or wanted as a member of society. This can create a hunger so great that people who find themselves locked into this situation become motivated to acquire a sense of power and purpose without regard for the impact of what they do on the lives of others. Crime and revolution are the sons and daughters of this kind of reaction.

As things now stand, some of the highest rates of unemployment are to be found among the youth of our land. Part of this unemployment is due to failure to coordinate schooling with the needs of the marketplace. It also is due to the fact that generations of Americans have been conditioned to think that the only prestige worth striving for is that which is based on the acquisition of money, material goods and power over others. Almost lost from sight are the honor, personal gratification and peace of mind that can be derived from being of service by helping others.

Human service jobs can be rewarding to the server and the served alike. In this day when so many people have found it impossible to obtain personal assistance of any sort, there must be many opportunities for people of all ages to establish home assistance, repair and handiwork agencies. Properly designed, these could yield a better income and infinitely more personal satisfaction than can be derived from unemployment or welfare payments for doing nothing, and even from some of the depersonalized production-line jobs through which many people are earning their living today.

It certainly should not come as a surprise to many that we are paying a very high price for the shortcomings in American child-rearing which we have been outlining in this treatise. We have hinted at some of these without giving specific figures. For instance, it has been observed that approximately 20 percent of pregnancies are unplanned and unwanted at conception. In many instances these are pregnancies of persons who are ill-prepared to become parents because of poverty, lack of education and extreme youthfulness. Included among these are many of the approximately 340,000 illegitimate births and 65,000 teenage abortions which have been taking place annually in recent years. The cost of prenatal care and delivery and maintenance of an infant at minimally adequate levels for the first year of life amounts to about $630. Thus, the cost of the illegitimate births alone is adding up to over $200 million  a year. By expending approximately $174 million a year in order to make family planning information and materials available to low-income families, our federal government is averting somewhere between 707,000 and 826,000 unwanted births. If it were not for this help, Americans would be paying via federal taxes in excess of $500 million a year just for prenatal care, delivery and the maintenance of such infants for just their first year of life. This represents a dollar savings-to-cost ratio of better than 2.5 to 1.

Planned Parenthood likewise estimates that the savings-to-cost ratio derived from federal reimbursement of legal abortions among medically indigent mothers who do not wish to carry their pregnancies through to term is at least 7 to 1. These figures are of interest both in respect to the initial costs inherent in having a child who is unwanted and in regard to the fact that it is much less expensive to prevent something than it is to cure it. All this is quite apart from the psychosocial benefits derived from these measures. We know of nothing more tragic or fraught with risk of human pain, suffering and waste than giving birth to a baby who is not really wanted by his parents. Some of the pain is felt by adults, but most is suffered by the children themselves. Many of these children are, as Mia Pringle has said, "born to fail" because of circumstances beyond their control.

Mental retardation comprises another commonplace disorder, the costs of which can be estimated in fiscal, as well as human, terms. There are now more than six million people in the United States who are considered to be mentally retarded. Of these, about 2.5 million are under twenty years of age. One quarter of all these cases can be linked to genetic, infectious and accidental causes for which there are as yet no effective preventive or curative measures. On the other hand, the other three quarters can be traced to inadequacies in prenatal and perinatal health care, nutrition, child-rearing and social and environmental opportunities. The President's Panel on Mental Retardation observed in 1962 that "a number of experiments with the education of presumably retarded children from slum neighborhoods strongly suggests that a predominant cause of mental retardation may be lack of learning opportunities and absence of 'intellectual vitamins' under these adverse environmental conditions."

In Massachusetts, it costs about two thousand dollars a year to provide a child who is at risk of mental subnormality for environmental reasons with supplementary support in the form of professionally staffed nursery school enrichment programs, day care centers and coordinated parent-teacher cooperative schemes. Lacking this, if the child fails to progress satisfactorily, the costs of managing a mentally handicapped child amount to between $2,500 and $8,700 per year. From the time they reach their eighteenth birthday, mentally incompetent individuals are carried for life by the United States Department of Public Welfare at a maintenance cost of about two thousand dollars per year. All this adds up to a maintenance bill of at least ninety-four thousand dollars per person by the time each reaches his or her sixty-fifth birthday. This deficit often is doubled in consequence of the reality that many of these people are not only dependent, but also incapable of working and earning.

Juvenile delinquency comprises another tragic outgrowth of the social and technological changes that have displaced so many children and adults. Between 1960 and 1973, according to the Federal Bureau of Investigation, arrests of children under eighteen years of age for murder increased by 201 percent, rape by 132 percent, robbery by 299 percent and assault by 206 percent. During the same period, arrests for burglary rose 104 percent, for larceny 124 percent and auto theft 51 percent. Arrests for forgery also increased 105 percent, for fraud 205 percent, for receiving stolen property 529 percent, for prostitution 286 percent, for drunken driving 201 percent and for breaking narcotic laws 4,673 percent. These increases averaged out to be approximately three times greater than those observed for adults during the same period.

By 1973, according to FBI records, the total of child arrests for criminal actions of various sorts had reached 1,717,366! These comprised more than one-quarter of all arrests recorded for persons of all ages. Moreover, these arrests were for major crimes; of all the arrests made, juveniles accounted for 11 percent of those for killing, 36 percent for armed robbery and 20 percent of those for rape. They also accounted for 17 percent of arrests for aggravated assault, 54 percent of those for burglary, 56 percent of those for automobile thefts and 48 percent for larceny thefts.

One out of every six American boys is referred to juvenile court before he reaches adulthood. If the present trend continues, 40 percent of the boys in this country will be apprehended and taken into court at least once in their lives for something other than traffic offenses. Relatively few of the youth who are arrested are sent to prison. However, of those who are sent to prison and subsequently released, nearly three-quarters are picked up again within six years. This is in keeping with the fact that most criminals are repeaters. This rising tide of juvenile delinquency will be swelling the ranks of adult criminals for years to come unless something is done to reverse these trends very soon.

It is estimated that about 43 percent of American families are victims of the approximately five and a half million crimes currently perpetrated every year. As of 1971, one of these occurs every 5.58 seconds. There is a burglary every 13 seconds, a larceny every 17 seconds, an auto theft every 94 seconds. A violent crime is taking place every 40 seconds, someone is forcibly raped every 13 minutes and every half hour someone is murdered.

Whether we are one of the immediate victims or not, the total monetary costs to us as citizens are stupendous. In 1970, they amounted to $51 billion. By 1973, the costs had risen to $83 billion a year. Everybody — except the perpetrators — pays this bill in hard-earned cash through property loss and damage, taxes that support the law enforcement and justice systems, the costs of insurance and special protection devices and the medical care required to heal injuries inflicted by criminals. We also pay a heavy toll in anxiety and well-founded fear of being robbed or assaulted as we walk the streets and traverse the parks in certain sections of our megalopolises, and even some of our superficially peaceful suburban and rural areas.

We have spelled out some of these costs in considerable detail because we realize that many Americans are business-minded and as such are concerned with deficits versus profits, assets versus liabilities and investments for growth. If one accepts as valid the costs outlined above, even the most reluctant among us may agree that it is imprudent to allow a large proportion of those who are destined to become the next generation of citizens, the fathers and mothers of our nation, to develop along such undesirable lines.

The section which follows will be devoted to outlining some of the steps which we as citizens could take to get at the roots of these problems in constructive ways. In doing so, we are not promising that funds and human effort expended along these lines will cure our problems within a short period of time. They are too widespread, too complex and deepseated, for that to be a realistic possibility. On the other hand, we are hoping that they will be viewed as investment possibilities with a large potential for gain to every member of our society, young and old alike.

*Recommendations for action.* Our nation pays a lot of lip service to health, welfare and safety as human rights that should be protected to the fullest extent possible, but has taken few steps to assure that children are nurtured and protected during the crucial years when they are too young to stand up for themselves. As a society, we have accepted the need for laws and regulations designed to assure that the air we breathe, the water we drink and the food we eat are safe. We welcome requirements that those who operate our airplanes, build our houses, care for us when we are sick and protect our legal rights when we are in trouble be properly trained and licensed to perform these roles. We accept government regulations of national defense, roadways and airways, interstate commerce and narcotics, as well as of our justice, education and welfare systems. With some grumbling we consent to government invasion of privacy in respect to our income, our physical and sometimes our emotional condition if we wish to teach in schools, to pilot passenger airplanes or to handle the food that other people eat. Our loyalty as citizens is investigated if we wish to work in positions of public trust. With respect to our children, we require premarital blood tests for venereal disease in an attempt to protect those who may be conceived, and we insist that silver nitrate solution be dropped in the eyes of newborn babies to guard against gonorrheal conjunctivitis. Some states require that newborns be tested for phenylketonuria so that children who have this disorder can be protected against mental retardation by being placed on special diets during infancy. We have, however, been reluctant to set up any system to assure that they are reared under conditions at least minimally adequate to the task. From the time an infant leaves the hospital after birth until he enters school, no physical or psychosocial check of any kind is required. Even though we know that the early years of a child's life have an extremely important bearing on his later development, we are so inured to the idea that parents are entitled to total control over their children's lives that we fail to protect even the basic interests of children for adequate environmental support, care and guardianship.

The superficial physical examination required when a child enters school usually is designed to do little more than insure that he has been immunized, has no contagious diseases or chronic conditions which might make his participation in school activities risky, and has no sight or hearing deficits that will interfere with his ability to learn. Aside from child labor laws designed to protect children against exploitation, no positive protective measures come into play unless the child is reported as being neglected or abused or gets himself into trouble by running away or violating the law. These measures are too little and too late. They often are activated only after a lot of damage has been done, when both physical and behavioral maladies have had time to become deepseated and are difficult to correct.

If children are to be protected during their early years from physical, psychological and social problems that can spell disaster for the rest of their lives, some program must be devised to identify those who are at risk before they have gotten into trouble. This program must also trigger corrective and supportive actions while they may serve as preventive rather than as therapeutic measures. It must reach all children, for neglect, deprivation, abuse, physical disease, psychological damage, mental retardation, delinquency and so forth are by no means limited to the children of any single social or economic level.

What is needed is a universal child-family screening and support program centered around a national health plan and having the following characteristics:

*One.* It should be geared in a benevolent and supportive way.

*Two.* It should identify major deficiencies in the child's social and material environment, starting as close to the onset of pregnancy as practicable and carrying through to the point where the child is reasonably self-sufficient. It should ascertain whether there is available an affectionately disposed and committed, capable parental person of some sort.

*Three.* It is essential to know whether the "parent(s)" have been rendered incapable of serving the needs of the child because they themselves are physically or mentally handicapped or unwell, are socially starved, overburdened, uneducated and inexperienced as regards children's needs, or unable because of poverty to buy enough of the right kinds of food to eat, clothes to wear or housing to live in. In the same vein, it is necessary to make sure that the family has access to medical attention, to playgrounds, and to day care and emergency-relief caretaker facilities and other essential resources.

*Four.* The children themselves should be screened for physical, intellectual, behavioral and emotional problems, particularly those for which corrective measures have been developed and are potentially available. It also should be determined whether these problems are being attended to, and if not, why not.

*Five.* In order that it may be applied universally to all American families with children, the child-family screening program should be directed by a federal "Child-Family Advocacy

Bureau" with branches scattered throughout all the communities of the nation. While the responsibility should thus be centralized, the manner in which the program is implemented should be adaptable to local circumstances insofar as they are compatible with a universal standard of excellence. At the local level, these branch agencies should mediate their screening and supportive services through a cadre of people specifically prepared for these tasks. It has been found that many of them can in fact be performed well by lay persons who, on the one hand, have been specifically trained in the necessary skills and who, on the other, are respected and trusted by the community in which they are working. These people should work under the direction of, and with the back-up of, a team comprised basically of a pediatrician, an educator and a psychologist. Representatives of other essential human services should be available as necessary. In short, they should be capable of functioning as the final common path through which all resource necessities could be identified, developed, funded and made available to those in need.

The strictest confidentiality would have to be maintained with respect to records on individual families. No material should be passed on in any form that would label the child or his family in ways detrimental to their privacy or to the attitudes of teachers, social workers and other persons towards them. In addition, parents should have access to the records on themselves and their dependent children, and a mechanism would have to be available for removing unjustly damaging material.

Though it is essential that responsibility for the guidelines, standards and funding of this program be centralized in a federal agency, it is also important that a strong effort be made to avoid the creation of another unnecessarily huge or expensive federal bureaucracy. It has been demonstrated at the state level that one way to do this is by developing contracts with certified, competent private agencies, whose services can be purchased by the government to perform certain specified tasks on its behalf and in accordance with its goals and standards. For example, the Commonwealth of Massachusetts has contracted with the Society for the Prevention of Cruelty to Children to serve the needs of children who are at risk of parental neglect or are known to have been abused. It does essentially the same thing with the New England Home for Little Wanderers. Likewise, the federal government has mediated many of its "Children and Youth" and "Maternal and Infant Care" programs via fully qualified non-profit private institutions. These, in turn, have often been able to adapt their efforts to local customs and requirements by involving respected, competent residents.

*Six.* In order to provide a continuous series of nationwide profiles of the status of families and children, after all clues which could tie information to particular families have been deleted, the coded records should be subjected to computer-based analysis of key variables. The resultant statistical material, issued annually, should be distributed to a "Child-Family Advocacy Bureau." It should be in a form which is useful for program planners, implementors and evaluators. Finally, this bureau should be responsible for, and supported in, the development of programs and services on the basis of needs identified in the statistical summaries. These should be coordinated with each other and with all existing public and private agencies concerned with children.

Despite the heroic efforts of agencies and organizations such as the federal Children's Bureau and the Child Welfare League of America, programs on behalf of children remain widely scattered, so that their accessibility and effectiveness are far less successful than they should be. Once we marshal available resources and fill in the gaps, we will find we have come a long way toward assuring that every child will be adequately cared for and protected.

In recognition of the fact that this is a large undertaking with many implications and ramifications, it would seem sensible to initiate it by setting up small-scale models in representative communities across the land. Because of hesitation on the part of some even to consider a benevolent screening and aid program, it may be useful to take advantage of existing laws, rules and regulations which permit and, indeed, require that representatives of authorized service agencies explore home situations surrounding children who have been found to be neglected, abused,

mentally or scholastically subnormal or delinquent in their behavior. We strongly suspect that explorations via any of these
portals would yield basically similar findings pertaining to gaps
in resources and services. We also believe that most families
would take advantage spontaneously of facilities which have been
made available in attractive form and free from financial barriers.

It is imperative that all these efforts be aimed first and fore-
most at fostering *health and competence.* They should not be
directed solely, or even primarily, at curing *disease and disability*
in classic ways. This seems by far to be the most promising way
to reduce the costs of medical care, education, discipline, job
training and so forth to minimum levels. Paradoxically, it also
appears to be the best way to achieve generations of healthy,
competent people who are able to enjoy life and, at the same time,
build and maintain a strong and secure homeland.

If these needs of children are to be met, grass-roots citizen
efforts must be brought to bear on national policies in ways that
will produce a rich harvest of action. To do this, we must recognize why our present efforts are missing the mark. There appear
to be several reasons.

First, there is the aforementioned traditional reluctance to
intervene in people's private affairs. When we do intervene, we
do it too late and too little.

Secondly, we have focused programs too much on children
from economically and socially disadvantaged families. There are
many fallacies to this approach. Singling out families in one
socioeconomic class automatically creates a two-class system of
services. It also unnecessarily labels and demeans the families
who receive the services. What is more, as we have noted several
times previously, many of the problems children have are not
limited to the poor and the disadvantaged but affect members of
all socioeconomic classes. It is false optimism to assume that
children will get the care and attention they should have just
because their parents are financially able to pay for services or
are highly educated. For one thing, parents in need of help or
guidance may be reluctant to seek it. For another, many necessary
community resources and services are not as yet available even

to those who have the ability to pay for them. All this is important, among other things, because most major programs must be tax-supported at least in part. People are often either indifferent or hostile to the idea of giving any support, either political or financial, to programs which yield them no direct personal return.

A third reason why our recent efforts are missing the mark is that many programs are categorical rather than comprehensive. Mechanisms for linking them with each other are tenuous. Categorical programs are essential. Childhood leukemia, child abuse and mental retardation, for example, will not be solved by a scattershot approach. Neither will they be solved by an approach that focuses only on one aspect of the problem. Each has social, medical, psychological and economic components, and they need to be dealt with in the round. Resources of many kinds and the knowledge represented in many disciplines must be brought to bear on the problems in a coordinated manner.

Fourth, a lot of programs get bogged down in their own bureaucratic red tape and in the vested interests of the armies of people who make careers out of administering richly funded programs. Too often, the result is that disproportionate amounts of the available funds go into administration and into the pockets of the administrators, leaving few of the benefits to filter through to the people the programs are designed to serve.

Fifth, the pages of recent history are littered with records of short-lived programs funded briefly from public or foundation monies and then allowed to die. This has happened partly because of the pressures of premature evaluation and partly because of fickle political winds that shift for the benefit of public relations impact, regardless of the crippling effects on promising programs. It has also happened because of the myth that if a government agency or a foundation funds a model program for two or three years, some community group or a guardian angel will appear out of nowhere to pick up future tabs and keep the program going. It isn't that simple. The budgets of most communities are already stretched to the breaking point, and excellent programs may have to be abandoned regardless of how badly they are needed. Leaving the well-being of the nation's children to chance borders on criminal negligence, and some system must be devised to assure long-term commitment to meeting their needs.

One has to recognize for what they are the endless bureaucratic excuses which may be presented by those who do not want to act. Marian Edelman has garnered more than a dozen examples of these. Paraphrased to fit our present purposes, they are:

1. *We're expert* — "You do not understand the complexities of the problem; we know best."

2. *Agency denial* — "I deny that any children are being excluded from services or that we are incorrectly labeling them or classifying them. Prove it."

3. *The exception* — "The examples you gave me are exceptions. Prove to me that these are widespread."

4. *Priorities* — "I admit the facts, but feel you have not presented a problem that is that important."

5. *Confession and avoidance* — "I admit the facts and feel very concerned, but there are overriding considerations which free *me* from any responsibility for acting to solve the problems."

6. *Improper jurisdiction* — "I understand the problem but I feel that it is not the responsibility of my agency. It is the task of the family and other institutions."

7. *Prematurity of request* — "We have known all along about these things that were happening, and we have made plans to correct the situation. Our efforts must be given a chance."

8. *Generalized guilt* — "What you say is true, but other agencies have similar problems and we are no worse than they are."

9. *Improper forum* — "The problem is really in the hands of the local or the federal government [depending upon which you are talking to] and there is little that we can do."

10. *Recrimination* — "I admit that there are children in trouble, but it is their own fault. It would not happen if they and their parents really cared."

11. *Further study* — "The problem has been referred to the proper officials for further study and we hope to develop a plan some time in the future."

12. *Community resistance* — "The community will not accept

it. *We* would like to make changes, but the attitudes and responses in the community would not let it work."

13. *Funding* — "There is no money."

Obviously, we had better be prepared to meet these arguments head on if we hope to make any progress.

## CONCLUDING REMARKS

People comprise the single most important resource of any and all nations. If the people are physically well, intelligent and skilled, and live in accordance with sensible ethical principles, the chances that a nation will thrive are maximal. In contrast, societies made up to a large extent of people who are physically unhealthy, intellectually undeveloped, unskilled, overly numerous, or amoral in behavior are at risk of eventual disorganization and demise.

If what we have just said is true, it is only prudent to make as sure as one can that all children are born wanted and needed, and society should insure to the fullest extent possible that they will become assets to the nation as they grow into adult responsibility.

For many reasons, most of which are understandable and excusable up to the point where one wakes up to what is happening, our nation seems to have lost sight of these fundamental realities. As a result, we are paying an ever higher price in the form of unwanted births, unattended and abused infants and children, undereducated and unskilled people, seriously destructive antisocial behavior, apathy and so forth.

As a nation we can eliminate these forms of disability, waste and suffering. But to do this, we are going to have to give child-rearing a much higher position in our national hierarchy of priorities than we are now giving it. We are also going to have to take the stand that it is imprudent to leave to chance how our children are being cared for during the years when they are dependent. This is why we have suggested that a universal benevolent screening and support system of some sort be created. We also suggest that once a child is born, his welfare should be the decisive factor, and the rights and wishes of adults in general, and of parents in particular, should be considered relative to this. For this, we need to have a nonprofit, nonpolitical national child advocacy bureau.

America may be slow to react to seemingly obvious threats, but once aroused, it has repeatedly demonstrated a remarkable capacity to attain desired objectives. Our hope is that this and its companion volume may serve to alert others to what seems to us to be the single most critical problem facing our country today — namely, to give child-rearing the priority it must have in our national affairs both publicly and privately if our nation is to continue to have the inner strength and competence needed to cope with the ever pressing challenges of life in an increasingly complex world.

# Some Supplementary Readings

Bremmer, Robert H. *Children and Youth in America: A Documentary History.* 3 vols. Cambridge, Mass.: Harvard University Press, 1970.

Bronfenbrenner, Urie. *Two Worlds of Childhood: U.S. and U.S.S.R.* New York: Russell Sage Foundation, 1970.

Child Care Resource Center. *A Family Day Care Study.* Cambridge, Mass.: Child Care Resource Center, 1972.

Children's Defense Fund of the Washington Research Project, Inc. *Children Out of School in America.* Cambridge, Mass.: Children's Defense Fund of the Washington Research Project, Inc., 1974.

Department of Health, Education and Welfare. *The CDA Program: The Child Development Associate.* Washington, D.C.: U.S. Government Printing Office, 1973

Department of Health, Education and Welfare. *Federal Programs for Young Children: Review and Recommendations.* 3 vols. Washington, D.C.: U.S. Government Printing Office, 1973.

Jencks, Christopher. *Inequality.* New York: Basic Books, 1972.

Kagan, Jerome. *Understanding Children.* New York: Harcourt, Brace, Jovanovich, 1971.

Keller, Helen. *The Story of My Life.* Garden City, New York: John Wiley and Sons, 1954.

Kempe, C. Henry, and Ray E. Helfer. *The Battered Child.* 2d ed. Chicago: University of Chicago Press, 1974.

Kohlberg, Lawrence. *Research in Moralization: The Cognitive-Developmental Approach.* New York: Holt, Rinehart and Winston, 1972.

Lesser, Gerald S. *Children and Television: Lessons from Sesame Street.* New York: Random House, 1974.

Meadows, Donnella H., *et al. The Limits to Growth: A Report for the*

*Club of Rome's Project on the Predicament of Mankind.* New York: Universe Books, 1972.

Minuchin, Salvador. *Families and Family Therapy.* Cambridge, Mass.: Harvard University Press, 1972.

Museum of Science. *Life in the Balance.* Boston: Museum of Science, 1973.

National Commission on Resources for Youth. *New Roles for Youth in the School and the Community.* New York: Citation Press, 1974.

Newman, Joseph, ed. *Crime in America — Causes and Cures.* Washington, D.C.: U.S. News and World Report, 1972.

Ohlin, Lloyd E. *A Situational Approach to Delinquency Prevention.* Washington, D.C.: U.S. Government Printing Office, 1970.

O'Toole, James. *Work in America: Report of a Special Task Force to the Secretary of Health, Education and Welfare.* Cambridge, Mass.: The Massachusetts Institute of Technology Press, 1973.

Packard, Vance. *A Nation of Strangers.* New York: David McKay Company, Inc., 1972.

Pringle, Mia Kellmer. *Able Misfits.* London: Longman Group Ltd. in association with National Children's Bureau, 1971.

*Profiles of Children: 1970 White House Conference on Children.* Washington, D.C.: U.S. Government Printing Office, 1970.

Richmond, George H. *The Micro-Society School: A Real World in Miniature.* New York: Harper and Row, 1973.

Roby, Pamela, ed. *Child Care — Who Cares?* New York: Basic Books, 1973.

Sarson, Evelyn. *Action for Children's Television.* New York: Avon Books, 1971.

Sidel, Ruth. *Women and Child Care in China.* Baltimore: Penguin Books, 1973.

Schorr, Alvin L. *Poor Kids.* New York: Basic Books, 1966.

Steinfels, Margaret O'Brien, *Who's Minding the Children?* New York: Simon and Schuster, 1973.

Talbot, Nathan B., ed. *Raising Children in Modern America,* vol. I. *Problems and Prospective Solutions,* Boston: Little, Brown and Company, 1976.

Talbot, Nathan B., and Mary C. Howell. "Social and Behavioral Causes and Consequences of Disease among Children." In *Behavioral Science in Pediatric Medicine,* ed. by Nathan B. Talbot, Jerome Kagan, and Leon Eisenberg; pp. 1–89. Philadelphia: W. B. Saunders Company, 1971.

United States Senate Committee on Finance. *Child Care Data and Materials.* Washington, D.C.: U.S. Government Printing Office, 1974.

Whiting, Beatrice B. and John W. M. *Children of Six Cultures.* Cambridge, Mass.: Harvard University Press, 1975.

Wilson, Edward O. *Sociobiology — The New Synthesis.* Cambridge, Mass.: Harvard University Press, 1975.

*Youth: Transition to Adulthood.* Report of the Panel on Youth of the President's Science Advisory Committee, James S. Coleman, Chairman. Chicago: University of Chicago Press, 1974.

Contributors to the Seminar

*Margaret Adams, M.A.*
Consultant in Social Work to the Interdisciplinary Program, Walter E. Fernald State School, Belmont, Massachusetts
Field: social work

*Duane F. Alexander, M.D.*
Assistant to the Scientific Director, National Institute of Child Health and Human Development, National Institutes of Health, Bethesda, Maryland
Field: child health and federal care programs

*Joel Alpert, M.D.*
Professor and Chairman, Department of Pediatrics, Boston University and Boston City Hospital
Fields: general pediatrics; family medicine

*Judith Assmus, M.A.*
Child Development Monitor and Researcher, Washington Research Project, Children's Defense Fund, Washington, D.C.
Field: child development

*Allan C. Barnes, M.D.*
Vice President, Rockefeller Foundation, New York City
Field: medicine in relation to population policy

*Ann Barnes, M.D.*
Assistant Clinical Professor of Obstetrics and Gynecology, Harvard University
Fields: reproductive physiology; clinical obstetrics and gynecology

*Daniel Bell, Ph.D.*
Professor of Sociology, Harvard University
Field: sociology of postindustrial society

*Bernard Berelson, Ph.D.*
President, Population Council, New York City
Fields: sociology; population control

*Garrett Birkhoff, Ph.D.*
Professor of Pure and Applied Mathematics, Harvard University
Field: pure and applied mathematics

*Joan Bissell, Ed.D.*
  Assistant Professor of Education, Harvard University
  Field: human development

*Sissela Bok, Ph.D.*
  Lecturer, Simmons College; Research Fellow in Medical Ethics, Harvard
  University
  Field: medical ethics

*T. Berry Brazelton, M.D.*
  Associate Professor of Pediatrics, Harvard University; Chief, Child De-
  velopment Unit, Children's Hospital Medical Center, Boston
  Fields: general pediatrics and child development

*Stephen Breyer, LL.B*
  Professor of Law, Harvard University Law School
  Fields: law, politics; public administration

*Urie Bronfenbrenner, Ph.D.*
  Profession of Psychology, College of Human Ecology, Cornell University
  Fields: psychology; family life

*Peggy Charren*
  President, Action for Children's Television
  Field: mass media — television and children

*Patsy Benjamin Cipolloni, M.D.*
  Instructor in Pediatrics, Harvard University; Assistant in Pediatrics, Massachusetts General Hospital; Director of Pediatrics, MGH Chelsea Community Health Center, Chelsea, Massachusetts
  Fields: general pediatrics; pediatric neurology

*Henry Steele Commager, Ph.D.*
  Lecturer in History, Amherst College
  Field: family structure

*Robert E. Cooke, M.D.*
  Former Professor of Pediatrics and Chairman of the Department of
  Pediatrics, Johns Hopkins University; Vice Chancellor, Center for Health
  Sciences, and Professor of Pediatrics, University of Wisconsin
  Field: general pediatrics

*John Drabik*
  Director, Exhibits Division, Museum of Science, Boston
  Field: child and family education programs

*Frederick J. Duhl, M.D.*
  President and Director, Boston Family Institute
  Field: child and family welfare

*Gunnar Dybwad, D. Juris.*
  Professor of Human Development, Brandeis University
  Field: handicapped children

*Arthur J. Dyck, Ph.D.*
   Professor of Population Ethics, Harvard University
   Field: ethics and religion

*Robert H. Ebert, M.D.*
   Professor of Medicine and Dean, Faculty of Medicine, Harvard University
   Fields: adult medicine; medical administration

*Marian Wright Edelman, LL.B.*
   Director, Children's Defense Fund of the Washington Research Project,
   Cambridge, Massachusetts
   Field: child advocacy

*Clifford W. Falby*
   Executive Director, New England Home for Little Wanderers, Boston
   Field: child welfare

*Carolyn French*
   Director, Child Advocacy Project, Roxbury Model Cities Program, Boston
   Field: child advocacy

*Paul A. Freund, LL.B.*
   University Professor and Senior Fellow, Society of Fellows, Harvard University
   Fields: law; ethics

*Sydney S. Gellis, M.D.*
   Professor and Chairman, Department of Pediatrics, Tufts University
   School of Medicine; Pediatrician-in-chief, New England Medical Center
   Hospital, Boston Floating Hospital for Infants and Children
   Field: general pediatrics

*Samuel Y. Gibbon, Jr.*
   Lecturer on Education, Harvard University; Executive Producer, *Sesame
   Street* and *The Electric Company,* Children's Television Workshop
   Field: mass media — television and children

*Peter Goldmark*
   Former Secretary, Massachusetts Office of Human Services
   Field: public provision of human services

*George Gustafson, Ph.D.*
   Assistant Director, National Institute of Education, Washington, D.C.
   Field: public policy in education

*Andrew D. Guthrie, Jr., M.D.*
   Assistant Professor of Pediatrics, Harvard University; Director, MGH
   Bunker Hill Health Center, Charlestown, Massachusetts
   Fields: ambulatory pediatrics; adolescent medicine; street youth coun-
   seling

*Matina S. Horner, Ph.D.*
    President, Radcliffe College
    Field: psychology and social relations

*Mary C. Howell, M.D., Ph.D.*
    Assistant Professor of Pediatrics and Associate Dean for Women, Faculty
    of Medicine, Harvard University
    Fields: developmental psychology; family care

*David Ives*
    President, WGBH-TV, Boston
    Fields: mass media; administration

*John E. Jackson, Ph.D.*
    Assistant Professor of Government, Harvard University
    Field: public administration

*Charles A. Janeway, M.D.*
    Former Pediatrician-in-chief, Children's Hospital Medical Center, Boston;
    Professor of Pediatrics, Harvard University
    Field: child health and development

*Christopher Jencks, Ed.M.*
    Associate Professor of Education, Harvard University
    Fields: sociology; education

*A. Sidney Johnson III*
    Staff Director, Subcommittee on Children and Youth, Committee on Labor
    and Public Welfare, United States Senate
    Field: child advocacy

*James M. Jones, Ph.D.*
    Assistant Professor of Social Psychology, Harvard University
    Field: social psychology

*Jerome Kagan, Ph.D.*
    Professor of Developmental Psychology, Harvard University
    Field: developmental psychology

*Francis Kelly, Ph.D.*
    Professor of Education, Boston College
    Field: delinquency

*C. Henry Kempe, M.D.*
    Professor of Pediatrics and former Chairman of the Department of
    Pediatrics, University of Colorado
    Fields: pediatrics; child abuse

*Edmund V. Keville, LL.B.*
    Associate Justice of the United States Appeals Court, Boston
    Field: child abuse

*Nathan Keyfitz, Ph.D.*
> Professor of Demography and Sociology, Harvard University
> Fields: demography; sociology

*Lawrence Kohlberg, Ph.D.*
> Professor of Education and Social Psychology, Harvard University
> Fields: education; social psychology

*Florence Ladd, Ph.D.*
> Associate Professor of City Planning, Harvard University
> Field: urban planning

*Walter V. Leefman, A.C.S.W.*
> Assistant General Secretary, Children's Protective Services, Boston
> Field: prevention of cruelty to children

*Pauline M. Leet, Ph.D.*
> Director, Bureau of Curriculum Services, Department of Education, Commonwealth of Pennsylvania
> Field: curriculum development

*Gerald S. Lesser, Ph.D.*
> Professor of Education and Developmental Psychology, Harvard University; associated with *Sesame Street*, Children's Television Workshop
> Fields: developmental psychology; mass media — television and children

*Richard Light, Ph.D.*
> Associate Professor of Education, Harvard University
> Fields: education; politics

*John Littlefield, M.D.*
> Former Professor of Pediatrics, Harvard University; Professor of Pediatrics and Chairman of the Department of Pediatrics, Johns Hopkins University
> Field: general pediatrics

*George C. Lodge, Ph.D.*
> Professor of Business Administration, Harvard University
> Field: business administration

*Charles U. Lowe, M.D.*
> Scientific Director, National Institute of Child Health and Human Development, National Institutes of Health, Bethesda, Maryland
> Fields: pediatrics; nutrition; health care delivery

*Diane Lund, LL.B.*
> Assistant Professor of Law, Harvard University Law School
> Fields: women and the law; family law

*Elizabeth McCormick, Ph.D.*
> President, Manhattanville College
> Fields: psychology; administration

*Jerome G. Miller, D.S.W.*
> Director, Illinois Department of Children and Family Services
> Field: correctional measures for delinquency

*Patricia Minuchin, Ph.D.*
> Professor of Psychoeducational Processes, Temple University
> Field: psychoeducational processes

*Salvador Minuchin, M.D.*
> Professor of Child Psychology and Pediatrics, University of Pennsylvania;
> Director, Child Psychiatric Service in Children's Hospital; Director, Child
> Guidance Clinic of Philadelphia
> Field: child and family psychiatry

*Hugo Moser, M.D.*
> Professor of Neurology, Harvard University; Neurologist, Massachusetts
> General Hospital; Superintendent, Walter E. Fernald State School, Bel-
> mont, Massachusetts
> Field: pathophysiology of mental retardation

*David S. Mundel, Ph.D.*
> Assistant Professor of Public Policy and Research Associate, Harvard Uni-
> versity
> Field: public policy

*John F. Mungovan, A.C.S.W.*
> Commissioner, Massachusetts Commission for the Blind, Boston
> Field: the handicapped

*J. Robert Nelson, Th.D.*
> Professor of Systematic Theology and Dean, School of Theology, Boston
> University
> Field: ecumenical theology

*Lloyd E. Ohlin, Ph.D.*
> Professor of Criminology, Harvard University Law School
> Field: criminology

*Vance Packard, M.S.*
> Author
> Field: sociology

*Orlando Patterson, Ph.D.*
> Professor of Sociology, Harvard University
> Field: Caribbean studies

*Thomas C. Peebles, M.D.*
> Associate Clinical Professor of Pediatrics, Harvard University; Pediatrician
> and Assistant Chief of Children's Service, Massachusetts General Hospital
> Field: general pediatrics

*Guido Perera, LL.B.*
  Lawyer, Hemenway and Barnes, Boston; former Chairman of the Board
  at Eastern Utilities Association
  Fields: law; trusteeship

*Justine Wise Polier, J.D.*
  Director, Children's Defense Fund, New York City
  Field: juvenile justice

*Ernesto Pollitt, Ph.D.*
  Associate Professor of Growth and Development, Department of Nutrition
  and Food Sciences, Massachusetts Institute of Technology
  Field: nutrition

*Philip J. Porter, M.D.*
  Associate Professor of Pediatrics, Harvard University; Pediatrician, Mas-
  sachusetts General Hospital; Chief Pediatrician, Cambridge Hospital
  Field: general pediatrics

*William Porter, Ph.D.*
  Dean, School of Architecture and Planning, Massachusetts Institute of
  Technology
  Field: urban design and planning

*Don K. Price, LL.B.*
  Professor of Government and Dean, Faculty of Public Administration,
  Harvard University
  Field: public administration

*Mia Kellmer Pringle, Ph.D.*
  Director, National Children's Bureau, London, England
  Field: handicapped children

*Roger Revelle, Ph.D.*
  Professor of Population Policy and Director, Center for Population Studies,
  Harvard University
  Field: population policy

*George H. Richmond, Ed.D.*
  Director, Society School Project, Educational Development Center, New-
  ton, Massachusetts
  Field: education for modern living

*Julius B. Richmond, M.D.*
  Professor of Child Psychology and Human Development and Professor of
  Preventive and Social Medicine, Harvard University
  Fields: pediatrics; child psychology; social medicine

*G. Bruce Robinson, LL.B.*
  Special Justice, Boston Juvenile Court, Suffolk County Courthouse, Com-
  monwealth of Massachusetts
  Field: juvenile justice

*Saul R. Rosoff*
Acting Director, Office of Child Development, Department of Health, Education and Welfare, Washington, D.C.
Field: child development

*Mary Potter Rowe, Ph.D.*
Special Assistant for Women and Work to the President and Chancellor of Massachusetts Institute of Technology
Fields: economics; working mothers and child care

*Richard R. Rowe, Ph.D.*
Director, Program in Clinical Psychology and Public Practice and Lecturer on Education, Harvard University
Field: clinical psychology and public practice

*Hilton A. Salhanick, M.D., Ph.D.*
Professor of Obstetrics and Gynecology and Professor of Reproductive Physiology, Harvard University
Fields: reproductive physiology; obstetrics and gynecology

*Frank E. A. Sander, LL.B.*
Professor of Law, Harvard University Law School
Field: law and public administration

*Charles A. Sanders, M.D.*
Associate Professor of Medicine, Harvard University; General Director, Massachusetts General Hospital
Fields: adult medicine; medical administration

*Christopher Sarson*
Executive Producer, *Zoom*, WGBH-TV, Boston
Field: mass media — television and children

*Sheldon J. Segal, Ph.D.*
Vice President, Population Council, New York City
Field: implementation of family planning

*Robert Selman, Ph.D.*
Research Associate in Education and Lecturer on Education, Harvard University
Field: child development

*William C. Smith, LL.B.*
Staff Attorney, Washington Research Project, Children's Defense Fund, Washington, D.C.; Director of 1984 Medical Experimentation Project
Field: child advocacy

*Gilbert Y. Steiner, Ph.D.*
Director of Governmental Studies, Brookings Institution, Washington, D.C.
Field: child welfare

*John Stetson*
  Vice President and Head of Personnel, First National Bank of Boston
  Field: worker procurement, development and management

*Alan A. Stone, M.D.*
  Associate Professor of Psychiatry and Lecturer on Law, Harvard University Law School
  Field: law and psychiatry

*Jule M. Sugarman*
  Former Commissioner, Human Resources Administration, New York City; Chief Administrative Officer, City of Atlanta
  Field: child welfare

*Consuelo Tagiuri, M.D.*
  Clinical Assistant in Psychiatry, Harvard University
  Field: child psychiatry

*Renato Tagiuri, Ph.D.*
  Professor of Social Sciences in Business Administration, Harvard University
  Field: social science in business administration

*Nathan B. Talbot, M.D.*
  Professor of Pediatrics, Harvard University; Chief of Children's Service, Massachusetts General Hospital
  Fields: pediatrics; biosocial influences on child health and development

*Harold Thomas, Jr., S.D.*
  Professor of Civil and Sanitary Engineering, Harvard University
  Field: population control

*Phyllis A. Wallace, Ph.D.*
  Professor of Industrial Relations, Massachusetts Institute of Technology
  Field: industrial relations

*Richard Warden*
  Assistant Legislative Director, United Auto Workers, Washington, D.C.
  Fields: management; worker development

*Robert S. Weiss, Ph.D.*
  Associate Professor of Sociology in the Laboratory for Community Psychiatry, Department of Psychiatry, Harvard University
  Field: social issues and life organizations

*Leora Wood Wells*
  Science writer

*Leonard E. White*
  Liaison Officer, Harlow Development Corporation, Essex, England
  Field: urban planning and management

*Sheldon H. White, Ph.D.*
   Professor of Educational Psychology, Harvard University
   Field: educational psychology

*Blenda J. Wilson, A.M.*
   Associate Dean for Administration, School of Education, Harvard University
   Field: educational administration

*Willard Wirtz, LL.B.*
   President, The Manpower Institute, Washington, D.C.
   Fields: labor relations; education for work

*Peter Wolff, M.D.*
   Professor of Psychiatry, Harvard University
   Field: child psychiatric research

*Robert Wood, Ph.D.*
   President, University of Massachusetts
   Field: urban planning and administration

*Paul N. Ylvisaker, LL.D.*
   Professor of Education and Dean, Faculty of Education, Harvard University
   Fields: education; administration

# Ad Hoc Participants

1. *Berelson, The Value of Children*
   Sissela Bok
   Matina S. Horner

2. *Barnes, What Factors Limit the Number of People That Our Planet Can Support in a Manner Sufficiently Satisfactory to Make Life Worth Living?*
   A. Sidney Johnson III
   Roger Revelle
   Harold Thomas, Jr.

3. *Segal, Limiting Reproductive Potential*
   Ann Barnes
   Nathan Keyfitz
   Roger Revelle
   Hilton A. Salhanick

4. *Bok, Ethical Problems of Abortion*
   Ann Barnes
   Arthur J. Dyck
   Paul A. Freund
   John Littlefield

6. *Kagan, The Psychological Requirements for Human Development*
   Mary C. Howell
   A. Sidney Johnson III
   Elizabeth McCormick
   Blenda J. Wilson
   Peter Wolff
   Paul N. Ylvisaker

7. *Kohlberg, Children's Perceptions of Contemporary Value Systems*
   Robert E. Cooke
   Andrew D. Guthrie, Jr.
   J. Robert Nelson
   Don K. Price
   Peter Wolff

8. *Minuchin and Minuchin, The Child in Context*
   Frederick J. Duhl
   Andrew D. Guthrie, Jr.
   Mary C. Howell
   Pauline M. Leet
   Robert S. Weiss

9. *Sheldon White, Socialization and Education*
   Joan Bissell
   Henry Steele Commager
   John Drabik
   Andrew D. Guthrie, Jr.
   Walter V. Leefman
   Gerald S. Lesser
   Robert Selman
   Consuelo Tagiuri

10. *Bronfenbrenner, The Roots of Alienation*
    Andrew D. Guthrie, Jr.
    Mary C. Howell
    Julius B. Richmond

11. *Kempe, Child Abuse and Neglect*
    Sissela Bok
    Andrew D. Guthrie, Jr.
    Edmund V. Keville
    Walter V. Leefman
    Richard Light

12. *Pringle, Reducing the Costs of Raising Children in Inadequate Environments*
    Joel Alpert
    T. Berry Brazelton
    Sydney S. Gellis
    Julius B. Richmond
    Saul R. Rosoff

13. *Patterson, The Black Micropolis*
    Carolyn French
    Andrew D. Guthrie, Jr.
    Christopher Jencks
    James M. Jones

14. *Ohlin, The Prevention and Control of Delinquent Acts*
    Francis Kelly
    Jerome G. Miller
    Justine Wise Polier
    Frank E. A. Sander
    Alan A. Stone

15. *Sugarman, Governmental Programs as a Supplement to Family Life*
    Clifford W. Falby
    Andrew D. Guthrie, Jr.
    Julius B. Richmond

16. *Lowe and Alexander, Child Health and Federal Care Programs*
    Robert H. Ebert
    Ernesto Pollitt

17. *Mary Potter Rowe, That Parents May Work and Love and Children May Thrive*
    Sissela Bok
    Mary C. Howell
    Matina S. Horner

18. *Edelman, A Political-Legislative Overview of Federal Child Care Proposals*
    Judith Assmus
    Julius B. Richmond
    Richard R. Rowe
    William C. Smith
    Jule M. Sugarman
    Richard Warden

19. *Lesser, Education and the Mass Media*
    Peggy Charren
    Samuel Y. Gibbon, Jr.
    David Ives
    Christopher Sarson

22. *Wirtz, Education for Work*
    George C. Lodge
    Charles Sanders
    John Stetson
    Phyllis A. Wallace

23. *Leonard E. White, Forms of Urban Design Compatible with Healthy Living by Children and Their Families*
    Charles A. Janeway
    Florence Ladd
    Vance Packard
    William Porter
    Robert Wood

24. *Lodge, Ideological Transformation and Institutional Structures and Behavior*
    Daniel Bell
    Guido Perera
    George H. Richmond
    Julius B. Richmond
    Charles A. Sanders

25. *Richard R. Rowe, Toward the Development of Assistance Systems for Children*
   Diane Lund
   Salvador Minuchin
   Thomas C. Peebles
   Philip J. Porter
   Gilbert Y. Steiner

26. *Dybwad, What Should Be Our National Policy toward Handicapped Children?*
   Margaret Adams
   Patsy Benjamin Cipolloni
   Hugo Moser
   John F. Mungovan

27. *Mundel, Some More Thoughts on the Direction of Children's Policy*
   Garrett Birkhoff
   Peter Goldmark
   George Gustafson
   Andrew D. Guthrie, Jr.
   Consuelo Tagiuri